Economic study of
Oil and Gas
Well Drilling

By

Roshdy Ebrahim, Ph.D

Roshdy Ebrahim

Copyright © 2018 Roshdy Ebrahim

All right reserved

ISBN: 9781980691334

Preface

The hunt for hydrocarbons is one of the most fascinating pursuits engaged in by the human species. Its early history is replete with stories of doggedly persistent wildcatters, who hovered on the feather edge of financial ruin to drill for oil against virtually insurmountable odds, in areas where the most influential geologists agreed that there could not possibly be any oil.

The implementation of carbon capture and storage (CCS) at extraction sites could also increase cost, though presumably the cost would be lower than that resulting from the imposition of emissions penalties. Meanwhile, enhanced oil and gas recovery based on CO_2 injection would be potentially less expensive due to emissions offsets based on sequestered CO_2.

The oil, gas, and salt water occupied the pore spaces between the grains of the sandstones, or the pore spaces, cracks, and vugs of the limestones and dolomites. Whenever these rocks were sealed by a layer of impermeable rock, the cap rock, the petroleum accumulating within the pore spaces of the source rock, was trapped and formed the petroleum reservoir. However, when such conditions of trapping the petroleum within the source rocks did not exist, oil gas moved (migrated), under the effects of pressure and gravity, from the source rock until it was trapped in another capped (sealed) rock.

Gas, oil, and water segregate within the trap rocks, because of the differences in density. Gas, when existing, occupied the upper part of the trap and water occupied the bottom part of the trap, with the oil between the gas and water. Complete displacement of water by gas or oil never occurred. Some salt water stayed with the gas and/or oil within the pore spaces and as a film covering the surfaces of the rock grains; this water is known as the connate water, and it may occupy from 10% up to 50% of the pore volume.

But it was not until A.D. 1859 that exploration for oil and gas started in earnest, when the first oil well was drilled by Edwin Drake in northwestern Pennsylvania, United States (some quarters claim it started in 1846 in Azerbaijan). Since then, a lot of advancement took place in the field of oil exploration and production (E&P), and there has been a phenomenal growth in petroleum industry, making it one of the most important sectors in the world influencing global economy and life of the people across the planet.

PREFACE 3

INTRODUCTION 9

1. PREPARING TO DRILL 17
   1.1. DRILLING THE WELL 18
   1.2. A WELL TEST 19
   1.3. WELL TEST OBJECTIVES................................21

2. DRILLING ENGINEERING AND OPERATIONS ..23
   2.1. DRILLING SYSTEMS AND EQUIPMENT..............23
   2.2. DRILLING THROUGH ABNORMAL PRESSURES 26
   2.3. DRILLING PROBLEMS 28
   2.4. DRILLING, FRACTURING, AND PRODUCTION.....29
      2.4.1. First Well Leg Drilling in Saudi Arabia 30
   2.5. OPTIMIZATION MODELS FOR WATER MANAGEMENT...31
   2.6. DEEPWATER OIL AND GAS............................33
   2.7. NATURE OF OFFSHORE DISCHARGES 39
      2.7.1. Produced Water 39
      2.7.2. Drilling Waste 43
      2.7.3. Wastes that Require Handling During Site Abandonment............................49
   2.8. WELL CONFIGURATION 51

3. SITE PREPARATION.....................................52
   3.1. ONSHORE SITES 53
   3.2. OFFSHORE SITES 55
   3.3. SHALE SITE CONSTRUCTION 57
      3.3.1. Shale gas well drilling 65
      3.3.2. Water Management in Shale Gas System 74

4. PRIMARY PRODUCTION 76

- 4.1. POWER PLANT AND TRANSMISSION SYSTEM..........95
- 4.2. HOISTING EQUIPMENT...96
- 4.3. ROTATING EQUIPMENT...96
- 4.4. CIRCULATING SYSTEM..97

5. **DRILLING FLUIDS**..**100**
   - 5.1. OIL-BASE MUDS...101
   - 5.2. SHALE STABILIZATION BY OIL MUD.............103
   - 5.3. GAS (AIR) DRILLING FLUID.........................105
   - 5.4. APPLICATION OF NITROGEN........................105

6. **FRACKING TECHNOLOGY**...........................**109**

7. **DRILLING TECHNIQUES**..............................**113**
   - 7.1. TOP HOLE DRILLING..................................113
   - 7.2. INTERMEDIATE AND RESERVOIR SECTION......116
   - 7.3. DIRECTIONAL DRILLING.............................119
   - 7.4. HORIZONTAL DRILLING..............................123
   - 7.5. MULTILATERAL WELLS...............................126
   - 7.6. HORIZONTAL WELLS.................................127
   - 7.7. EXTENDED REACH DRILLING......................133
   - 7.8. SLIM HOLE DRILLING................................136

8. **WELL PLANNING AND COSTS**....................**139**
   - 8.2. WELL PLANNING......................................139
   - 8.2. COSTS OF DRILLING.................................141
   - 8.3. OPERATING COSTS..................................144
   - 8.4. OPERATING MARGIN................................145
   - 8.5. BUSINESS SEGMENTS..............................145

9. **CONTRACTS**..**148**
   - 9.1. TURNKEY CONTRACT................................150
   - 9.2. FOOTAGE CONTRACT................................150
   - 9.3. INCENTIVE CONTRACT..............................150
   - 9.4. DAY RATE CONTRACT...............................151

9.5. PARTNERING AND ALLIANCES 151
10. DRILLING RIG 154
    10.1. PLATFORM RIG 158
    10.2. JACKUP RIG 158
    10.3. SEMISUBMERSIBLES 159
    10.4. DRILLSHIP 161
    10.5. SUBMERSIBLE RIG 162
11. OFFSHORE RIG MARKETS 164
12. CONTRACT DRILLING MARKET 171
    12.1. NEWBUILD MARKET 175
    12.2. GEOGRAPHIC DISTRIBUTION 177
    12.3. CONTRACTS 180
    12.4. OWNERSHIP 182
        12.4.1. Public Firms 183
        12.4.2. State-Owned Firms 184
        12.4.3. Private Firms 185
        12.4.4. Market Share 186
    12.5. MARKET POWER 186
    12.6. RIG TIME LOSS AND NONPRODUCTIVE DRILLING TIME 187
13. BOREHOLE LOGGING 191
14. LOGGING/MEASUREMENT WHILE DRILLING (LWD/MWD) 194
    14.1. ORIGINATION OF WELL LOGGING 199
    14.2. WHAT IS WELL LOGGING? 200
    14.3. USE OF LOGS 202
    14.4. PRODUCTION LOGGING 203
15. THE ADVANCED WELL LOGGING TECHNOLOGY 206

- 15.1. ECLIPS-5700 WELL LOGGING SYSTEM..........206
- 15.2. EXCELL-2000 WELL LOGGING SYSTEM 207
16. INTEGRATED INTERPRETATION OF WELL LOGGING DATA 209
17. MUD LOGGING...212
18. WELL CORRELATION 217
19. PRODUCING THE WELL 225
20. THE ROLE OF DRILLED WELLS IN DEVELOPMENT 226
21. WELL COMPLETION 228
22. EXPLORING OBSERVED COGNITIVE ERROR TYPES IN TEAMS WORKING IN SIMULATED DRILLING ENVIRONMENTS 231
23. WELL ABANDONMENT 236
24. PRODUCTION SHUTDOWN 238
REFERENCES 244
BIOGRAPHY OF THE AUTHOR..............................248

Introduction

A revolutionary invention in 1909 greatly increased the depth of wells that could be drilled. The original drilling technology, adapted from water well drilling, was to drop a heavy "bit" onto the rock. The rock would shatter and be periodically removed by a scoop. This method is slow, inefficient and not feasible below a thousand meters or so. The far more efficient continuous hydraulic rotary drilling system used today was invented by Hughes Tool Co. c. 1900. It consisted of a rotary cutting tool at the bottom end of a pipe, which was rotated as a whole by an engine at the top. A lubricant was pumped down from above, both to cool the drill and to carry the cuttings back to the surface outside the pipe. This enabled the drill to operate continuously, except for pauses to add new sections of pipe at the top. Depth was virtually unlimited. [1]

After 1920, most wells were drilled with the hole full of heavy mud to prevent the early-day blowouts and gushers. However, the heavy mud makes it possible to drill right through a productive oil reservoir and never know about it. An exact measure of the percentage of oil, or of natural gas, in a rock was desperately needed. The answer came, not from

---

[1]Robert Ayres: ENERGY, COMPLEXITY AND WEALTH MAXIMIZATION. Springer International Publishing Switzerland 2016. P 274: 275

Schlumberger or its competitors, but from GusE Archie at Shell. Archie first published his method in 1941, but exploration for new oil was sidelined during World War II in favor of all-out production from existing fields.

In 1947, a Shell exploratory well at Elk City, Oklahoma, was about to be plugged and abandoned as a dry hole. Gus Archie argued that his calculations showed a zone that would produce oil. The company history records that "after some discussion" a test was made of the suspect zone. It did produce oil; that well and the surrounding 136 wells in the Elk City oil field have produced 600 million barrels of oil and are still producing today. The 1947 discovery initiated an orgy.

For the next few years, well logs from older "dry" holes were worked over with Archie's methods. Some of them did, in fact, indicate over- looked oil-saturated horizons. It was easy hunting; sometimes you could even drill out the cement plug and use the original borehole.

Archie actually discovered two relationships, sometimes called Archie's first law and Archie's second law.6 His first law gives a relationship between the electrical resistance of a water sample and the resistance of a rock with its pore space saturated with the same water.

His second law shows how the electrical resistance is changed as oil substitutes for the water. The two laws are combined into a simple equation known, obviously, as the Archie equation.7 Gus Archie was my manager when I worked at the Shell research lab. It's great for morale to have a living legend on the team. Imagine being a rookie in the Yankee dugout and watching DiMaggio step up to the plate. There are lots of good scientists in the world and very few good managers of science. Archie was both. [1]

The next major step was catalytic cracking. Eugene Houdry was the prime mover. In 1927, by trial and error (like Edison) he finally discovered an effective cracking catalyst consisting of oxides of aluminum and silicon.

With support from Vacuum Oil Co. (later Socony-Vacuum and finally Sun Oil Co). Houdry got the first catalytic cracking process operational in 1937. It processed 12,000 bbl/day and doubled again the yield of gasoline by the Burton process to 50 %. By 1940 there were 14 Houdry fixed-bed catalytic plants in operation, processing 140,000 bbl/day. Shortly after that a moving bed "Thermofor catalytic cracking" process (or TCC) was put into operation in 1943 and by 1945 it was processing 300,000 bbl/day

---

[1]K E N N E T H S . D E F F E Y E S: Hubbert's Peak. Princeton University Press. 2001. P 75: 76

into high octane gasoline for the war effort. The so-called fluid catalytic cracking process (FCC) in use today was developed by a consortium of companies led by Exxon, primarily to by-pass the Houdry patents. Success was achieved quite rapidly, thanks to a suggestion by two MIT professors, Warren K. Lewis and Edwin Gilliland, for fluidizing the catalyst itself. This turned out to be successful, and now all refineries use some version of the FCC process. [1]

On October 3, 1930 wildcatter "Dad" Joiner and self-educated geologist "Doc" Lloyd (with financial help from H.L. Hunt) discovered the huge East Texas field.

This discovery was disastrously ill-timed. During 1931 an average of eight wells per day were being drilled in East Texas, resulting in a huge glut. The surplus was exacerbated by declining demand due to the depression. The price dropped to an all-time low of 10 cents per barrel, far below cost. During that year the Texas Railroad Commission tried to limit output to 160,000 bbl/day, but actual output at the time was 500,000 bbl/day. This restriction was toothless and was ignored.

---

[1] Robert Ayres: ENERGY, COMPLEXITY AND WEALTH MAXIMIZATION. Springer International Publishing Switzerland 2016. P 275

However, the governor of neighboring Oklahoma, William Murray—who had the same problem—put all the wells in the state under martial law, from August 11 1931 until April 1933.

There after the Texas Railroad Commission (TRC) took over the task of regulating output, bringing it down to 225 bbl/day per well. The price gradually recovered as the economy recovered, but the TRC set world prices until OPEC took over in 1972. It is worthy of note that the energy content of the oil produced, in those distant days, was well over 100 times the energy required to drill the wells and transport the oil. Today the return on energy invested in oil drilling is around one fifth of that, taking a world-wide average, and the energy return on some of the newer "alternatives" (such as ethanol from corn) is around one twentieth, or less, of what it was in 1930.

The year 1933 was also when Socal (now Chevron) got the first license to explore for oil in Saudi Arabia. California-Arabia Standard Oil Co (Casoc) was created, and Texaco joined Casoc in 1936. The first strike was at Dharan in 1938.

The Ras Tanura refinery (world's largest) started operations in 1945. In 1948 Esso and Mobil bought into Casoc and the name was changed to Arabian-American Oil Company

(Aramco). That was when the world's largest oil field, Ghawar (still not exhausted) was discovered. It was the peak year for discovery. In 1950 King Abdul Aziz threatened nationalization and agreed to a 50–50 split of the profits. The US government gave the oil companies a tax break called the "Golden Gimmick" equal to the amount they had to give Saudi Arabia. The Trans-Arabian pipeline (to Lebanon) began operations. Aramco confirmed the size of Ghawar and Safaniya (biggest offshore field) in 1957. The whole story of the search for "black gold" is told very well in "The Prize". [1]

The earliest forms of oil and gas wells were actually pits dug by hand. Numerous examples from 500 BCE to 1800 CE from Europe, the Middle East, India, Southeast Asia, and Japan are described by Owen. Well drilling appears to have originated in China, where a heavy cylindrical weight was used for impact drilling and bamboo was used for well casing. The target was brine for manufacture of salt, which was important for food preservation as well as flavoring and was a highly regulated commodity. Wells were 100 m deep by 600 BC and reached 1000 m deep by 1100 CE. Natural

---

[1] Robert Ayres: ENERGY, COMPLEXITY AND WEALTH MAXIMIZATION. Springer International Publishing Switzerland 2016. P 276

gas was initially a byproduct, although it was often used as a fuel for evaporating brine.

Natural gas seeps and eternal flames are found around the world. They often became sites or religious temples. Others, such as Burning Springs near Niagara Falls became a tourist attraction about 1800. In 1825, the nominally first U.S. natural gas well was dug in Fredonia, N.Y., where the gas was used for lighting downtown. However, contemporary brine wells near Charleston, W. Va., were also dealing with problems and benefits of co-produced oil and gas, and brine wells were reaching 600 m depth.

Although Colonel Drake's 1859 well in Oil Creek, Pennsylvania, is commonly thought to be the first well drilled specifically for oil, it was actually preceded the year before by one in Oil Springs, Ontario, a couple years before that by an oil mine in Poland, and a few years before that by a well in Baku, Asia. Nevertheless, the Pennsylvania discovery led to the Rockefeller monopoly and fortune within 20 years. Crude oil continued its rise at the turn of the 20th century. Winston Churchill saw the future and converted the British naval fleet after World War I.

Gasoline, which was a waste product from making lighting oil, became the most popular petroleum product in the 20th century with the advent of the automobile. [1]

---

[1] Alan K. Burnham: Global Chemical Kinetics of Fossil Fuels. Springer International Publishing AG 2017. P 7

1. PREPARING TO DRILL

Once the site has been selected, it must be surveyed to determine its boundaries, and environmental impact studies may need to be performed. Lease agreements, titles, and right-of way accesses for the land must be obtained and evaluated legally. For offshore sites, legal jurisdiction must be determined. Once the legal issues have been settled, the crew goes about preparing the land; preparation is essential and involves the following steps:

1. L and is cleared and leveled, and access roads may be built.

2. Because water is used in drilling, there must be a source of water nearby. If there is no natural source, a water well is necessary.

3. Reserve pit, which is used to dispose of rock cuttings and drilling mud during the drilling process and which is lined with plastic to protect the environment, is created. If the site is an ecologically sensitive area, such as a marsh or wilderness, then the cuttings and mud must be disposed offsite, it may have to be trucked away instead of being placed in a pit.

Once the land has been prepared, several holes must be dug to make way for the rig and the main hole. A rectangular pit (a cellar) is dug around the location of the actual drilling hole. The cellar provides a workspace around the hole for the workers and drilling accessories. The crew then begins drilling the main hole, often with a small drill truck rather than the main rig. The first part of the hole is larger and shallower than the main portion and is lined with a large-diameter conductor pipe. Additional holes are dug off to the side to temporarily store equipment, after which the rig equipment can be brought in and set up. [1]

1.1. Drilling the Well

Well drilling has gone through major developments of drilling methods to reach the modern method of rotary drilling. In this method, a drilling bit is attached to the bottom end of a string of pipe joints known as the drilling string. The drilling string is rotated at the surface, causing rotation of the drilling bit. The rotation of the bit and the weight applied on it through the drilling string causes the crushing and cutting of the rock into small pieces (cuttings). To remove the cuttings from the hole, a special fluid, called the drilling fluid or the drilling mud, is pumped down through the drilling string, where it exists through nozzles in the bit as jets of fluid. This fluid cleans the bit from the cuttings and carries the cuttings to the surface through the annular space between the drilling string and the wall of the hole. At the surface, the mud is screened to remove the

---

[1] James G. Speight: The Chemistry and Technology of Petroleum. FOURTH EDITION. Taylor & Francis Group, LLC. 2007. P 140

cuttings and is circulated back into the drilling string. The drilling operation is performed using huge and complex equipment known as the drilling rig. [1]

1.2. A well test

During a well test, a transient pressure response is created by a temporary change in production rate. The well response is usually monitored during a relatively short period of time compared to the life of the reservoir, depending upon the test objectives. For well evaluation, tests are frequently achieved in less than two days. In the case of reservoir limit testing, several months of pressure data may be needed.

In most cases, the flow rate is measured at surface while the pressure is recorded downhole. Before opening, the initial pressure P_i is constant and uniform in the reservoir. During the flowing period, the drawdown pressure response Δp is defined as follows: [2]

---

[1] Hussein K. Abdel-Aal Mohamed A. Aggour Mohamed A. Fahim: Petroleum and Gas Field Processing. Second Edition. Taylor & Francis Group, LLC. 2016. P 14: 15
[2] JOHN CUBITT: Handbook of Petroleum Exploration and Production. E l s e v i e r Science B.V. 2002. P 1

$$\Delta p = p_i - p(t)$$

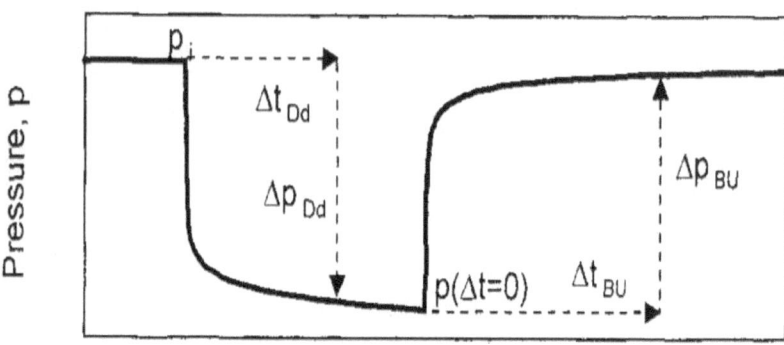

When the well is shut-in, the build-up pressure change Δp is estimated from the last flowing pressure p(Δt=0):

$$\Delta p = p(t) - p(\Delta t = 0)$$

The pressure response is analyzed versus the elapsed time Δt since the start of the period (time of opening or shut-in). [1]

1.3. Well test objectives

Well test analysis provides information on the reservoir and on the well. Geological, geophysical and petrophysical information is used where possible in conjunction with the well test information to build a reservoir model for prediction of the field behavior and fluid recovery for different operating scenarios. The quality of the communication between the well and the reservoir indicates the possibility to improve the well productivity. Usually, the test objectives can be summarized as follows:

Exploration well: On initial wells, well testing is used to confirm the exploration hypothesis and to establish a first production forecast: nature and rate of produced fluids, initial pressure and well and reservoir properties. Tests may be limited to drill stem testing only.

Appraisal well: The previous well and reservoir description can be refined by testing appraisal wells to confirm well productivity, reservoir heterogeneities and boundaries, drive mechanisms etc. Bottom hole fluid samples are taken for PVT laboratory analysis.

---

[1] JOHN CUBITT: Handbook of Petroleum Exploration and Production. E l s e v i e r Science B.V. 2002. P 2

Longer duration testing (production testing) is usually carried out.

Development well: On producing wells, periodic tests are made to adjust the reservoir description and to evaluate the need for well treatment, such as work-over, perforation strategy or completion design, to maximize the well's production life. Communication between wells (interference testing), monitoring of the average reservoir pressure are some usual objectives of development well testing. [1]

---

[1] JOHN CUBITT: Handbook of Petroleum Exploration and Production. E l s e v i e r Science B.V. 2002. P 2

2. Drilling Engineering and Operations

Following the preparation stage of field development (i.e., setting the production strategy, determining the locations of the wells in the field, and designing the well completions), the drilling-related activities begin. The drilling program is first designed. Then, plans are prepared and executed to acquire the required equipment and materials. The drilling sites in the field are then prepared for the equipment and materials to be moved in, and the drilling operations begin. Depending on the organization of activities within the oil company, drilling engineers may only be responsible for drilling and casing of the well, and production engineers will be responsible for completion of the well. Alternatively, drilling engineers may be responsible for drilling and completion of the wells.

The drilling program consists of three main stages: (1) drilling the hole to the target depth, (2) setting the various casings, and (3) cementing the casing.

2.1. Drilling Systems and Equipment

Whether onshore or offshore drilling is carried out, the basic drilling system employed in both the cases will be the rotary rig. The parts of such a unit and the three basic functions carried out during rotary drilling operations are as follows:

- Torque is transmitted from a power source at the surface through a drill string to the drill bit.

- A drilling fluid is pumped from a storage unit down the drill string and up through the annulus. This fluid will bring the cuttings created by the bit action to the surface, hence clean the hole, cool the bit and lubricate the drill string.

- The subsurface pressures above and within the hydrocarbon-bearing strata are controlled by the weight of the drilling fluid and by large seal assemblies at the surface (BOPs).

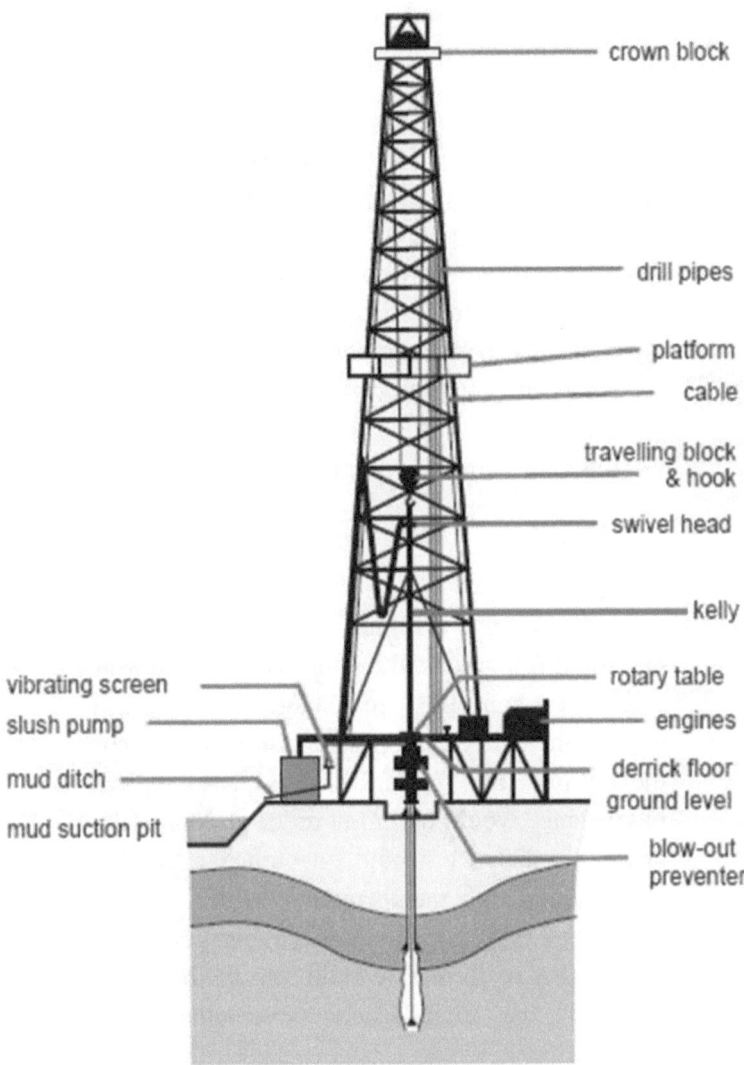

However, in practice, onshore and offshore drilling units are often quite different in terms of technology and degree of automatization. This is largely driven by rig availability, costs and safety considerations, and will be explained in more detail in the following text.

We will now consider the rotary rig in operation, visiting all elements of the system. The type of rig operation described first is now found mainly in low-cost onshore areas. For complicated, more expensive wells, older rigs have usually been upgraded to include a top drive system and automated pipe handling as described later in this section. New rigs are usually built with this equipment as standard. [1]

2.2. Drilling through abnormal pressures

When drilling through normally pressured formations, the mud weight in the well is usually controlled to maintain a pressure greater than the formation pressure to prevent the influx of formation fluid. A typical overbalance would be in the order of 200 psi. A larger overbalance would encourage excessive loss of mud into the formation, which is both costly, and may damage the reservoir properties. If an influx of formation fluid into the borehole did occur due to insufficient overbalance, the

---

[1] Frank Jahn, Mark Cook and Mark Graham: HYDROCARBON EXPLORATION AND PRODUCTION. 2ND EDITION. Elsevier B.V. 2008. P 52: 53

lighter formation fluid would reduce the pressure of the mud column, thus encouraging further influx, and an unstable situation would occur, possibly leading to a blowout. Hence, it is important to avoid the influx of formation fluid by using the correct mud weight in the borehole.

When drilling through a shale into an over pressured formation, the mud weight must be increased to prevent influx. If this increased mud weight would cause large losses in shallower, normally pressured formations, it is necessary to isolate the normally pressured formation behind casing before drilling into the over pressured formation. The prediction of overpressures is therefore important in well design.

Similarly, when drilling into an under pressured formation, the mud weight must be reduced to avoid excessive losses into the formation. If the rate of loss is greater than the rate at which mud can be made up, then the level of fluid in the wellbore will drop and there is a risk of influx from the normally pressured overlying formations.

Again, it may be necessary to set a casing before drilling into under pressures. [1]

---

[1] Frank Jahn, Mark Cook and Mark Graham: HYDROCARBON EXPLORATION AND

2.3. Drilling Problems

Problems can be encountered in the drilling of any hole at any time; and drilling personnel must be aware of this fact and of the symptoms that indicate the various types of problems. On the other hand, many problems can be avoided or minimized by proper planning. Geological information and the experience gained from drilling previous wells in the same area can be used to predict the existence of problem zones, and such data should certainly be used to the fullest extent. However, problems encountered in one well may not exist in the immediate vicinity, while new problems can arise at any time. Such is the nature of drilling a small hole to great depths through often heterogeneous layers of subsurface rock. [1]

The major types of problems to be discussed here include loss of circulation, abnormal pressures and blowouts, sloughing formations, crooked holes, stuck drill pipe, and the control of formation fluids. Although discussed separately, many of these conditions are closely interrelated, and measures taken to prevent or ameliorate one may have an aggravating effect on others. Therefore, they

---

PRODUCTION. 2ND EDITION. Elsevier B.V. 2008. P 136: 137

([1])Ellis H.Austin: Drilling Engineering, International Human Resources Development Corporation • Boston D. Reidel Publishing Company, 1983. P 58

must be considered as an ensemble both in well planning and during the actual drilling operation. [1]

2.4. Drilling, Fracturing, and Production

After the shale site construction, the drilling rig is moved on site and assembled. A conductor hole is predrilled, and then conductor pipes are inserted to prevent soft rocks from caving and conduct drilling mud from bottom to the surface during drilling process. Depending on the number, depth, and length of horizontal wells to be drilled, the drilling stage can last for a few months, which requires a constant supply of drilling fluid and proper handling of sediments and wastewater. Once the drilling is completed, protective casing and cementing are used. [2]

The following stage is the well completion, which mainly involves the hydraulic fracturing operation. A mixture of water, sand, and chemical additives is injected underground at a high pressure to break up shale-rock formations, such that fractures are created and held open by proppant, and then shale gas and

---

[1]Ellis H.Austin: Drilling Engineering, International Human Resources Development Corporation • Boston D. Reidel Publishing Company, 1983. P 58
[2]Georgios M. Kopanos · Pei Liu Michael C. Georgiadis: Advances in Energy Systems Engineering. Springer International Publishing Switzerland 2017. P 25

oil can be extracted. Typically, the horizontal wells are stimulated by stages, depending the specific fracturing schedule and technology applied, the hydraulic fracturing stage could last for several months. Once fracturing is completed, a wellhead is constructed, and the local gathering pipelines are prepared for the controlled extraction of natural gas. [1]

2.4.1. First Well Leg Drilling in Saudi Arabia

The well was planned as a vertical exploration well to target the prognosed Cretaceous, Jurassic and Triassic structural apexes within the NW-SE trending four-way dip closure.

Based on the seismic image, the stratigraphic units appeared to be of relatively uniform thickness across the structure except in the detachment levels where some lateral thickening may occur as a result of folding or faulting. Due to the geometry of the fold, shortening and degree of complexity were thought to increase with depth accordingly to the mechanical model described above.

The well was drilled to a total depth (TD) of 4511mMD/RT in the main hole. Extensive open-hole logging was conducted

---

[1]Georgios M. Kopanos · Pei Liu Michael C. Georgiadis: Advances in Energy Systems Engineering. Springer International Publishing Switzerland 2017. P 25

through the Cretaceous, Jurassic and Triassic sections. The 26" and 17 ½" sections penetrated the Tertiary and Cretaceous formations and encountered the tops in a range of ±15 m compared with the well prognosis. The 17 ½" phase ended in first meters of the Barsarin Fm. anhydritic levels. [1]

2.5. Optimization Models for Water Management

Most existing publications addressing water management problem focus on evaluating the environmental impacts of hydraulic fracturing and providing techno-economic analysis of specific water management options. However, considering the shale water supply chain as a complex system that involves numerous technology alternatives, it is important to develop an integrated approach to address all the challenges and opportunities of the water-energy system simultaneously. [2]

first propose an optimization model for shale gas water management. Key aspects for water use in hydraulic fracturing, including source water acquisition, wastewater production,

---

[1] François Roure • Ammar A. Amin Sami Khomsi • Mansour A.M. Al Garni: Lithosphere Dynamics and Sedimentary Basins of the Arabian Plate and Surrounding Areas. Springer International Publishing AG 2017. P 191
[2] Georgios M. Kopanos · Pei Liu Michael C. Georgiadis: Advances in Energy Systems Engineering. Springer International Publishing Switzerland 2017. P 31

reuse and recycle, subsequent transportation, storage, and disposal are considered. A discrete-time two-stage stochastic MILP model is proposed to address the uncertainty of water availability. In this work, two specific problems are considered. The first problem mainly focuses on the water acquisition stage, and the goal is to find the optimal water acquisition strategy regarding different water sources. The uninterruptible sources are available throughout the year but require expensive truck transportation. The interruptible sources can be transported by pipeline with lower cost but are affected by seasonal availability. Storage option is also taken into account to coordinate water acquisition and demand. The objective is defined as minimizing the expected trucking and pumping cost of the water required to complete all the well sites. According to the optimization results of an example case, the total expected cost is reduced by $2.4 million compared against a heuristic schedule. The second problem addresses a more comprehensive model, where the handling of wastewater and revenue from gas production are taken into account. The goal is to determine the optimal fracturing schedule, as well as logistics for water acquisition, flowback reuse, and treatment. The objective is maximizing the expected profit from shale gas production after considering the operating cost for water management. Through this optimization, the expected profit is increased by 37 % from $156.41 million to $214.15 million, and the total cost is reduced from $25.02 million to $23.41 million compared to the heuristic schedule. to optimize the long-term investment decisions using a deterministic MILP model. Multiple design decisions including capacity of water impoundments, pipeline options, treatment technologies and facility locations, as well as the fracturing schedule are addressed. [1]

2.6. Deepwater Oil and Gas

Production in the early days of the oil industry was exclusively onshore, but in due course eyes turned seaward to tap the extensions of fields lying on the coast. At first, that was achieved by deviating wells from the shore, and later, by drilling from steel platforms in shallow waters, as for example in Trinidad, Peru and Lake Maracaibo. Later, a rig was mounted on a barge that could be moved from location to location, which was pioneered in 1949 in the shallow waters of the Gulf of Mexico, off Louisiana.

The breakthrough then came with the idea of building the rig on two submerged pontoons that could rest in relatively tranquil water beneath the wave-base. The first such rig, *Blue Water No.1*, came into operation in 1962, and began to extend the range of drilling to as

---

[1] Georgios M. Kopanos · Pei Liu Michael C. Georgiadis: Advances in Energy Systems Engineering. Springer International Publishing Switzerland 2017. P 32

much as 200 m of water. The design was subject to continual improvement such that it soon became possible to drill routine wells in the stormy waters of the North Sea. There are two other types of offshore rig worth mentioning: the jack-up which sits on long retractable legs resting on the seabed; and the drillship, having a rig mounted mid-ships on an ordinary vessel, held in place by anchors or thrusters. [1]

Gradually, the continental shelves of the world were explored, and delivered some substantial finds both from the extensions of existing onshore basins and from entirely new provinces. Offshore seismic technology also saw great advances from the early days when a seismic boat let off explosive changes, the echoes of which bounced off formations far below the seabed to be recorded on receptors towed behind the vessel. New sources of energy were developed and computing power brought great sophistication, such that offshore surveys are now cheaper and give better results than onshore ones. Despite these advances, great challenges remain in installing the production facilities, such as the massive steel and concrete platforms of the North Sea.

As the opportunities of the continental shelves were gradually exhausted, attention

---

[1] C.J. Campbell: Campbell's Atlas of Oil and Gas Depletion. Colin J. Campbell and Alexander Wöstmann 2013. P 371

began to turn to the Deepwater domain. The Brasilian State Company, *Petrobras,* pioneered this development, as the country was facing the high cost of imports during the early 1980s. To its enormous credit, it successfully began to find and develop fields in exceptionally deep water. Parallel developments came in the Gulf of Mexico, and later off Angola, Nigeria and other countries on the other side of the South Atlantic. [1]

Offshore oil resource is playing an increasingly significant role in satisfying our fossil fuel needs. According to the U.S. Geological Survey, in 2014, about 47% of the total untapped oil resource comes from the sea. For the offshore oil industry, it is becoming an important issue to reliably supply electrical power to the offshore oil platforms.

At present, most of the oil platforms far from the land are powered by the independent power stations built on them. This power supply mode, however, would lead to blackout of the platform once the power station thereon shuts down. Therefore, it becomes a trend to construct offshore oilfield power systems that can interconnect every platform to improve the reliability of power supply.

---

[1]C.J. Campbell: Campbell's Atlas of Oil and Gas Depletion. Colin J. Campbell and Alexander Wöstmann 2013. P 371

Since 2010, offshore platforms have been connected electrically along the coast of China. Many larger-scale offshore power systems are emerging. Therefore, how to plan a highly reliable power system suitable for the offshore oilfield is critical for the construction as well as the effective and safe operation of the offshore oil industry. [1]

The technology of planning has been widely studied and applied to large-scale inland power systems for the past decades. Conventionally, the process of inland power system planning is divided into two steps, i.e., generation expansion planning (GEP) and transmission expansion planning (TEP), for the following reasons: It is difficult to deal with GEP and TEP simultaneously due to the huge number of variables. ` The construction of power stations and transmission lines are in the charge of different sections of the power industry. ´ Over 80% of the total expansion cost goes to GEP whereas TEP only accounts for a small fraction of the investment, which leads to relatively minor errors with the two-step planning procedure.

---

[1] Dawei SUN, Xiaorong XIE, Jianfeng WANG, Qiang LI, Che WEI: Integrated generation-transmission expansion planning for offshore oilfield power systems based on genetic Tabu hybrid algorithm. J. Mod. Power Syst. Clean Energy. 2017. P 117

Either GEP or TEP has been widely investigated in the past research. For GEP, different techniques have been used, for instance, fuzzy logic, genetic algorithm (GA), particle swarm optimization (PSO), Tabu search and etc. However, without the geographical information of generators and transmissions, all generators were just considered to be at a single nodal point. As for TEP, there are also different methods discussed in previous literature, for example, mixed integer linear programming (MILP) algorithms, heuristic methods, game theory and artificial intelligence techniques. Similarly, without clear information of generations, the obtained TEP result can hardly be the most cost-effective one.

However, the composite generation and transmission system expansion planning is reasonable for offshore oilfield power systems. Three reasons are explained for this idea. First, offshore systems are much smaller than inland systems and have far fewer stations and lines to be planned, which means the number of decision variables is much smaller. Second, both generation and transmission system are constructed and operated by a single company (In China, the company is China National Offshore Oil Corporation). As a result, simultaneous and integrated planning of generation and transmission is feasible in the perspectives of both technology and management. Last but not least, the investment cost of submarine cables is enormous enough to be comparable to that of generators.

Consequently, separate execution of TEP and GEP could lead to ill-considered decisions. Overall, integrated planning is not only feasible but also necessary for offshore oilfield power systems. Furthermore, special attention should be paid to two issues for the planning of offshore systems. One is the outage cost, which need be taken into account for the fact that loss of electricity in the offshore oilfield would cause serious damage to drilling equipment or even a complete halt of oil production. The other is the shipping cost, which should be explicitly considered for the reason that the distance from the mainland to offshore platforms is critical for determining the construction costs of generators and cables.

To address the above issues, an innovative planning method for offshore oilfield power systems is proposed in this paper. An integrated generation-transmission expansion planning model is proposed which includes outage cost and shipping cost. A genetic Tabu hybrid algorithm (GTHA) based optimization method has been developed to solve the integrated planning problem to find the optimal plan. [1]

2.7. Nature of Offshore Discharges
2.7.1. Produced Water

Produced water is the water generated from the oil and gas extraction process. It includes: the water native to the producing formation, water injected into the formation to increase reservoir pressure and to sweep oil from the formation and traces of various well treatment solutions and chemicals added during production and the oil/water separation process. The volume of produced water varies over the life cycle of an oilfield, typically increasing over time.

Formation water which comprises the bulk of the produced water, is found in the same rock formation as the crude oil and gas or an adjoining level of the same formation (e.g. below the oil/gas cap). Formation water is classified as meteoric, connate or mixed. Meteoric water comes from rain water that percolates through bedding planes and permeable layers. Connate water (seawater in which marine sediments were originally

---

([1])Dawei SUN, Xiaorong XIE, Jianfeng WANG, Qiang LI, Che WEI: Integrated generation-transmission expansion planning for offshore oilfield power systems based on genetic Tabu hybrid algorithm. J. Mod. Power Syst. Clean Energy. 2017. P 118

deposited) contains chlorides, mainly sodium chloride (NaCl), and dissolved solids in concentrations often many times greater than common seawater. Mixed water is characterized by both a high chloride and sulfate-carbonate-bicarbonate content, which suggests multiple origins.

Besides its ionic constituents, produced water may also contain dissolved and dispersed organic compounds, including hydrocarbons (both aliphatic and aromatic) oxygen, nitrogen and Sulphur containing compounds (e.g. carbon dioxide, hydrogen sulphide, ammonia and small quantities of heavy metals).

Normally formation water is low in sulphate ion and may contain significant quantities of calcium, barium and/or strontium ions. Produced water is usually in a reduced state and it may have both a significant chemical oxygen demand (COD) and biological oxygen demand (BOD).

Produced water is the water generated from the oil and gas extraction process. It includes: the water native to the producing formation, water injected into the formation to increase reservoir pressure and to sweep oil from the formation, and various well treatment solutions and chemicals added during production and the oil/water separation process. The volume of produced water varies over the life cycle of an oilfield, typically increasing over time.

Formation water, which initially comprises the bulk of the produced water, is found in the same rock formation as crude oil and gas, or in an adjoining level of the same formation (e.g. below the oil/gas cap). Formation water is classified as meteoric, connate or mixed. Meteoric water comes from rainwater that percolates through bedding planes and permeable layers. Connate water (seawater in which marine sediments were originally deposited) contains chlorides, mainly sodium chloride (NaCl), and dissolved solids in concentrations many times greater than common seawater. Mixed water is characterized by both chloride and sulfate carbonate- bio carbonate content, which suggests multiple origins.

Besides its ionic constituents, produced water may also contain dissolved and dispersed organic compounds, including hydrocarbons (both aliphatic and aromatic) oxygen, nitrogen and sulfur containing compounds, e.g. carbon dioxide, hydrogen sulfide, ammonia, and small concentrations of heavy metals. Normally formation water is low in sulfate ion and may contain significant quantities of calcium, barium and/or strontium ions. Produced water is usually in a chemically reduced state and it may have both a significant chemical oxygen demand (COD) and biological oxygen demand (BOD). It will react with air and changes in pressure and may release carbon dioxide or hydrogen sulfide, which can also cause chemical reactions in the water.

Treating chemicals are typically added to produced water and may significantly affect its environmental impact. These chemicals are used to accomplish several functions, including the following most common uses:

• Breaking emulsions to aid in the separation of oil and water

• Preventing the formation of water-formed scales

• Controlling the growth of bacteria in the producing wells and production system

• Aiding in the treating of water to remove oil

The industry magazine, World Oil, annually publishes a list of chemicals currently used in production treating applications. Specific information on the properties of these materials can be obtained from the suppliers' Safety Data Sheets (SDS). [1]

---

[1] Stefan Orszulik: Environmental Technology in the Oil Industry. Third edition. Springer International Publishing Switzerland 2016. P 223: 224

2.7.2. Drilling Waste

Drilling wastes include drilling fluids (or muds) and the formation fragments (known as cuttings) removed in the drilling process. Drilling fluids are suspensions of solids and other materials in a liquid base. The composition and properties of drilling fluids are determined by their functions. Three of the primary functions that drilling muds perform are:

• Lubricating and cooling the drilling bit

• Maintaining downhole hydrostatic pressure

• Cleaning out the hole by bringing cuttings to the surface

In order to work, muds must have a high density, a high viscosity and lubricity. To meet these requirements the muds, contain weighting agents such as barium sulfate (Barite) or ion (III) oxide to increase the density of the mud, clays (bentonite, etc.) or polymers to adjust viscosity and chemical to increase the mud properties. The industry magazine, World Oil, annually published a list of chemicals used in the formulation of drilling muds. Information on the properties of these materials can be obtained from their suppliers from their Safety Data Sheets (SDS). In recent years, great emphasis has been given to selecting mud components that both perform well and are environmentally friendly.

Drilling fluids fall into one the three classes based on the fluid comprising the mud:

• Water based muds

• Oil base muds

• Synthetic based muds

More than one type of mud may be used in a single well depending on the conditions encountered. A water-based drilling fluid or mud is one in which water is the continuous phase and the suspending medium for solids and other liquids, whether or not oil is present. Water based drilling muds are relatively inexpensive. Modern formulations are generally not-toxic to marine fauna. Discharged cuttings will disperse in the water column.

The water in water-based muds can be fresh or salt water. Clays or organic polymers are added to achieve the proper viscosity. Barite is added to achieve the correct mud weight (density), and other components are added to mud systems to create the desired characteristics. The United States Environmental Protection Agency (EPA) recognizes eight generic water-based mud types (OCS Guidelines).

Oil based drilling fluids are ones in which the continuous phase is oil: diesel, mineral or some other oil. Simplistically they can be viewed as water-based muds dispersed in oil. One important difference from water-based muds is that viscosity is achieved by emulsification of water in oil as well as through the use of clay. They are also more expensive to use that water-based muds.

Oil based drilling fluids are used to solve drilling problems that water based muds cannot handle efficiently, or at all. Conditions warranting the use of oil-based muds include: required thermal stability when drilling high-temperature wells, required specific lubricating characteristics when drilling deviated wells, the ability to reduce stuck pipe or hole wash-out problems when drilling thick, water-sensitive formations and drilling through water soluble formations such as salt. Most offshore wells fall into one or more of these classes.

Concerns over the potential toxicity of oil-based drilling fluids led to the development of synthetic based drilling muds (SBMs). Synthetic based muds are drilling fluids that use synthetic organic chemicals, principally containing carbon, hydrogen and oxygen, as base fluids. Synthetic based muds are more expensive than oil-based fluids but are more environmentally benign and have increasingly replaced the old oil-based muds. SBMs have low toxicity because of the elimination of the polynuclear aromatic hydrocarbons (PAHs). They were also designed to have faster biodegradability, lower bioaccumulation potential and, in some instances, less drilling waste volume. This means that the discharge of SBM cuttings may be permitted. Like oil-based drilling fluids, synthetic based fluids are hauled to shore after use to be reprocessed and reused.

Cuttings are small pieces of formation rock that are generated by the crushing action of the drill bit. Drill cuttings are carried out of the borehole by the drilling fluids. Drill cuttings themselves are inert solids from the formation. However, drill cuttings discharge also contain drilling fluids that adhere to the cuttings. The volume of the mud that adheres to the cuttings can vary considerably depending on the formation being drilled and the cuttings' particle size distribution. An old, but still valid general rule of thumb is that 5 % mud, by volume, is associated with the cuttings. In the case of some water-based drilling fluids, the formation materials drilled up will become part of the mud solids and chemical adjustments have to be made to accommodate them. This results in an increase in mud volume that is not needed in the drilling process. Some drilling mud then becomes a waste and must be disposed of. Therefore, drilling mud itself becomes a waste material in two ways: as a coating on cuttings and as excess mud.

Drilling fluids are designed to have the required characteristics to aid in the drilling of the well, while at the same time limiting their potential environmental impact. Their potential for environmental impact is partially determined by where they end up in the environment as well as their intrinsic properties. Water based mud and cuttings tend to disperse into the water column on discharge. The dispersion is broken and the solid components slowly settle to the sediment layer at the bottom of the sea. Because of the cuttings are rapidly dispersed and their liquid components diluted, their potential impact should be less than that of oil based, or synthetic muds, but spreads over a much wider area.

Cuttings from oil-based mud drilling have oil on their outer surfaces and do not tend to disperse in the water column. The solid components tend to settle rapidly to the bottom and collect in piles under the platforms of drilling rigs. Depending on water depth, free oil on the cuttings tends to rise to the surface of the water and spread over the surface of the water. The environmental impact of the cuttings tends to be highly localized initially and persist over a long time in the sediment and water column immediately above it. In addition to drilling muds, the offshore oil and gas industry uses a number of water-based fluids. These include:

• Completion fluids

• Packer fluids

- Workover fluids

Completion fluids are typically solutions of salts in water. They are used to clean out wells after drilling is complete and aid in the setting of downhole equipment.

Packer fluids are concentrated salt solutions placed between the tubing and the casing of a well. Their purpose is to hold pressure on the formation in case the packer fails. They must have a high density in order to be heavy enough to exert sufficient pressure on the producing formation. Workover fluids, such as hydrochloric acid, are used in cleaning, repairing, and stimulating wells. Typical operations include washing sand from the tubing or wellbore, fracturing water formed scales and corrosion products. The salts used to make these fluids include the cations of sodium, potassium, calcium, barium and zinc, and the anions of chloride, bromide and sulfate.

Completion fluids can be either transported offshore as water solutions, or alternatively the solid salt can be taken offshore and the solution prepared on-site.

Spills of completion fluids could result from broken flow lines on the platform or on boats, or from tank failures. When large volumes of completion fluids are needed they are generally transported on work boats. In the event that the vessel has an accident, the completion fluids could be released. [1]

2.7.3. Wastes that Require Handling During Site Abandonment

site abandonment has the potential for discharging materials to the sea. Platforms having large integral storage vessels might have residual oil or chemicals in the vessels; the presence of the platform or its residue modifies the local environmental habitat by its very existence. For example, most of the northern Gulf of Mexico is a mud bottomed body with few coral reefs or other bottom relief. Abandoned platforms will tend to act as artificial reefs and attract fish species that live around reefs.

Abandoned platforms could be hazardous to shipping or fishing boats. This would be especially troublesome if they were not visible from the surface. In the North Sea there is the additional problem of old cuttings piles beneath some of the older platforms. These piles resulted from drilling with oil-based muds during the period when discharge of such cuttings was allowed. The interior of these piles may be wet with oil and contain no continuous water. Degradation of these cuttings is

---

[1] Stefan Orszulik: Environmental Technology in the Oil Industry. Third edition. Springer International Publishing Switzerland 2016. P 224: 226

dependent on wind and wave action and bacterial degradation of any oil. Wind and wave action does not normally reach the bottom of the northern North Sea and with little water content the piles will not rapidly bacterially degrade.

Removing a platform without removing the cuttings piles would leave them as hazard to trawling and other activities for periods estimated to be up to 100 years.

There are a number of wastes that are generated as part of the abandonment process. These include wastes resulting from:

• Cleaning and purging vessels resulting in wastes including:

• scale

• tank bottoms

• wash water

• Seabed clean-up

These wastes have to be treated, handled and disposed of if they cannot be reused or recycled. [1]

---

[1] Stefan Orszulik: Environmental Technology in the Oil Industry. Third edition. Springer International Publishing Switzerland 2016. P 231: 232

2.8. Well Configuration

Wells may be drilled vertical, directional or horizontal. Branches spurred off from the original wellbore called sidetracks are often drilled to target different areas of a reservoir. Exploration wells are almost always drilled vertically with the target directly below the rig. Most developmental wells are drilled directionally because several wells targeting different zones and traps are drilled from a central location, or the target lies under salt or an environmentally sensitive area. Long horizontal sections may be required to tap thin beds far from the rig or heavy oils that require greater contact with the reservoir. The distance along the wellbore is referred to as measured or total depth while true vertical depth is measured from the surface straight down to the target. [1]

---

[1] Mark J.Kaiser, Brian F.Snyder: The Offshore Drilling Industry and Rig Construction in the Gulf of Mexico, Springer-Verlag London 2013. P 3

3. Site Preparation

Once the objectives of the well are clear, further decisions have to be made.

One decision will be where to site the drilling location relative to the subsurface target and which type of rig to use.

If no prior drilling activities have been recently carried out in the area, an environmental impact assessment (EIA) will usually be carried out as a first step. An EIA is usually undertaken to:

_ meet the legal requirements of the host country

_ ensure that the drilling activity is acceptable to the local environment

_ quantify risks and possible liabilities in case of accidents.

An EIA may have to include concerns such as:

_ protection of sites of special interest (e.g. nature reserves, archaeological sites)

_ noise control in built-up areas

_ air emission

_ effluent and waste disposal

_ pollution control

_ visual impact

_ traffic (rig transport and supply)

_ emergency response (e.g. fire, spills).

The EIA is an important document, often on the drilling project's critical path.

In new areas, the required environmental data may not be available. Data collection may stretch over several seasons to capture such parameters as currents, migration paths, breeding habitats or weather patterns. [1]

3.1. Onshore sites

A site survey will be carried out, from which a number of geotechnical parameters can be established, for example carrying capacity of the soil at the planned location, possible access routes, surface restrictions like built-up areas, lakes, nature reserves, the general topography and possible water supplies. The survey will allow the adequate preparation of the future location. For instance, onshore in a swamp area the soil needs to be covered with support mats.

The size of the rig site will depend on operational requirements and possible

---

[1]Frank Jahn, Mark Cook and Mark Graham: HYDROCARBON EXPLORATION AND PRODUCTION. 2ND EDITION. Elsevier B.V. 2008. P 60: 61

constraints imposed by the particular location. It will be determined by

_ the type of derrick or mast (which will depend on the required loads); it must be possible to rig this up on site

_ the layout of the drilling equipment

_ the size of the waste pit

_ the amount of storage space required for consumables and equipment

_ the number of wells to be drilled

_ whether the site will be permanent (in case of development drilling).

A land rig can weigh over 200 tons and is transported in smaller loads to be assembled on site.

Prior to moving the rig and all auxiliary equipment, the site will have to be cleared of vegetation and levelled. To protect against possible spills of hydrocarbons or chemicals, the surface area of a location should be coated with plastic lining and a closed draining system installed. Site management should ensure that any pollutant is trapped and properly disposed of.

If drilling and service personnel require accommodation at the well site, a camp will need to be constructed. For safety reasons, the camp will be located at a distance from the drilling rig and consist of various types of portacabins. For the camp, waste pits, access roads, parking space and drinking water supplies will be required. [1]

3.2. Offshore sites

The survey requirements will depend on rig type and the extent of the planned development, for example single exploration well or drilling jacket installation.

A typical survey area is some 4 by 4 km, centered on the planned location. Surveys may include:

_ Seabed survey: employing high-resolution echo-sounding and side scan sonar imaging, an accurate picture of the sea bottom is created. The technique allows the interpreter to recognize features such as pipelines, reefs and wreckage.

Particularly if a jack-up rig is considered, an accurate map of these obstructions is required to position the jack-up legs safely. Such a survey will sometimes reveal crater-like structures (pockmarks), which are quite common in many areas. These are the result of gas escape from deeper strata to the

---

[1]Frank Jahn, Mark Cook and Mark Graham: HYDROCARBON EXPLORATION AND PRODUCTION. 2ND EDITION. Elsevier B.V. 2008. P 61

surface and could indicate danger from shallow gas accumulations.

_ Shallow seismic: unlike 'deep' seismic surveys aimed at the reservoir section, the acquisition parameters of shallow surveys are selected to provide maximum resolution within the near-surface sedimentary layers (i.e. the top 800 m). The objective is to detect indications of shallow gas pockets or water zones. The gas may be trapped within sand lenses close to the surface and may enter the borehole if penetrated by the drill bit, resulting in a potential blowout situation. Gas chimneys are large-scale escape structures where leakage from a reservoir has created a gas-charged zone in the overburden. If shallow water zones are penetrated, they may flow to the surface of the seabed and reduce the loadbearing capacity of the conductor pile.

_ Soil boring: where planned structures require soil support, for example drilling jackets or jack-up rigs, the load-bearing capacity has to be evaluated (just like on a land location). Usually a series of shallow cores are taken to obtain a sample of the sediment layers for investigation in a laboratory.

Particularly for jack-up rigs, site surveys may have to be carried out prior to each re-employment to ensure that the rig is positioned away from the previously formed 'footprints' (depressions on the seabed left by the jack-up legs on a previous job). [1]

3.3. Shale Site Construction

First, potential shale wells are explored through geologic evaluation. Once a potential shale site is identified, the well operator needs to reach a lease agreement with the corresponding landowner and then obtain the drilling permits. It is the operator's responsibility to guarantee that all the following drilling and production activities will be carried out in accordance with relevant regulations. After the approval of the operator's permit by local environmental regulation agencies, the site construction and well drilling can start. [2]

The shale site is typically constructed following these steps: the first step involves the clearance of proposed area and the accommodation of equipment. Meanwhile, a road way is constructed to provide access to the shale site. Subsequently, pits/impoundments are constructed to properly handle the fluids during drilling and hydraulic fracturing. Next, pipelines associated with shale sites are installed,

---

[1] Frank Jahn, Mark Cook and Mark Graham: HYDROCARBON EXPLORATION AND PRODUCTION. 2ND EDITION. Elsevier B.V. 2008. P 61: 62

[2] Georgios M. Kopanos · Pei Liu Michael C. Georgiadis: Advances in Energy Systems Engineering. Springer International Publishing Switzerland 2017. P 24

including gathering lines, injection lines, and water supply lines. Other infrastructures such as storage tanks are built as well. [1]

The horizontal wells drilled in the direction perpendicular to the direction of maximum permeability (drilling in the direction of minimum horizontal stress, if permeability anisotropy is caused by stress anisotropy) may provide noticeably higher gas production rate compared to the wells that are drilled perpendicular to the direction of minimum permeability (drilling in the direction of maximum horizontal stress if permeability anisotropy is caused by stress anisotropy). [2]

The wells in the tight gas reservoir are drilled overbalanced using water-based mud and completed as cased-hole perforated wells. Analysis of the field and lab data showed that there are various possible explanations or combination of circumstances that may have contributed to the wells' poor productivities: [3]

---

[1] Georgios M. Kopanos · Pei Liu Michael C. Georgiadis: Advances in Energy Systems Engineering. Springer International Publishing Switzerland 2017. P 24

[2] Nick Bahrami: Evaluating Factors Controlling Damage and Productivity in Tight Gas Reservoirs. Doctoral Thesis. Springer International Publishing Switzerland 2013. P 30: 31

[3] Nick Bahrami: Evaluating Factors Controlling Damage and Productivity in Tight Gas Reservoirs. Doctoral Thesis.

• Vertical wells in low permeability gas reservoirs may not provide economical rates due to the very limited formation surface area that is open to the wellbore.

• The core data analysis (X-Ray diffraction) detected smectite which shows the reservoir rock is sensitive to water-based fluids. Drilling the wells overbalanced using water-based mud, may have caused significant damage and low productivity.

• In addition, perforation efficiency was low due to the reservoir rock tightness and also presence of the large wellbore breakouts behind casing filled by cement.

In the wells that are hydraulically fractured, the fracturing operations did not result in any improvement of productivity which might be due to:

• Job reports indicate that about 40 % of the water based treating fluids is not recovered. The formation is sensitive to water damage and the large leak-off of water into formation during fracturing might be one of the main factors that cause low productivity.

• Well production and test data also indicated that hydraulic fracture size is significantly

---

Springer International Publishing Switzerland 2013. P 48: 49

smaller than the expectations. The limited size hydraulic fractures may have caused the hydraulic fractures productivity to be low.

Even though it is generally agreed that a vast amount of resources are locked within these unconventional systems, the challenges for effective and economical production still seem daunting for the current state of technology. This is tied to the dearth of in-depth knowledge about the complexities of these systems and the lack of mathematical and analytical techniques that adequately capture them. Existing production techniques such as hydraulic fracturing, which is heavily used for shale and tight formations, have met with increasing concerns about their potential impact on the environment. In addition, this type of wells show productivity decline due to fracture closure with time and uncertainty of fracture propagation due to the lack of knowledge of formation stresses. Therefore, extensive effort has been directed towards developing effective alternatives for field development tools.

Advanced well structures (or multi-lateral wells) are defined as wells having one or more branches (laterals) tied back to a mother wellbore, which conveys fluids to or from surface. Technology of horizontal and multilateral fishbone wells provides significant leverage where conventional vertical wells cannot efficiently maintain a profitable development. The main advantages of these well configurations are to increase well productivity and reduce development cost per field. Multi-lateral wells can produce higher rates of oil and gas because they have a larger reservoir contact area compared to vertical wells.

Not only these wells produce more, but they also provide better sweep efficiency by mitigating or preventing gas and water comings as the position of the laterals within the producing layers provides enough distance to water and gas bearing zones. In addition, more reserves are realized due to the extended reach of multilateral wells which creates a larger drainage area. Consequently, a large field can be developed with less number of wells and therefore, multilateral wells can reduce time and costs of drilling and surface facilities construction operations. These well structures also reduce surface footprints by eliminating the need for multiple drilling pads whilst still effecting adequate surface area contact with the reservoir.

Advanced well structures have seen increased field application over the years. Joshi (2000) reported that over 700 multi-lateral wells have been drilled in Saskatchewan, Canada. Making a comparison with single lateral wells, Stalder et al. (2001) report that advanced well structures yield higher recovery factors because of the extra leverage gained from the ability to produce from multiple targets, thus sustaining the declining rates and keeping the well operationally feasible for longer periods. The various forms of multilateral wells such as stacked dual lateral, gullwing multi-lateral, crow's foot triple lateral, pitchfork dual lateral, and fishbone wells are drilled. The Figure shows two adjacent pad developed with a combination of stacked dual lateral, gullwing, crow's foot, and fishbone multilateral wells.

Advanced well structures have also been deployed in the Shaybah field of Saudi Arabia. Fish bone well (SHYB-220) was drilled with a total of eight laterals comprising an aggregate reservoir contact of 12.3 km as part of a pilot program. A production test on SHYB-220 indicated a PI of 126 STB/D/psi, which represents a six-fold increase compared to 1-km horizontal completions in similar facies (10 md). Furthermore, a four-fold reduction in unit-development costs was achieved. These well systems are particularly useful in producing from thin formations, formations with isolated pockets of producing zones, and unconventional reservoirs. Advanced well structures compare favorably with other well design options.

Yu et al. (2009) showed close comparison in net present value from development plans using fish bone well and hydraulic fractures. They founded that these two types of wells can generate comparable NPV values. They concluded that as the drilling technology develops, use of fishbone wells with increased number of rib

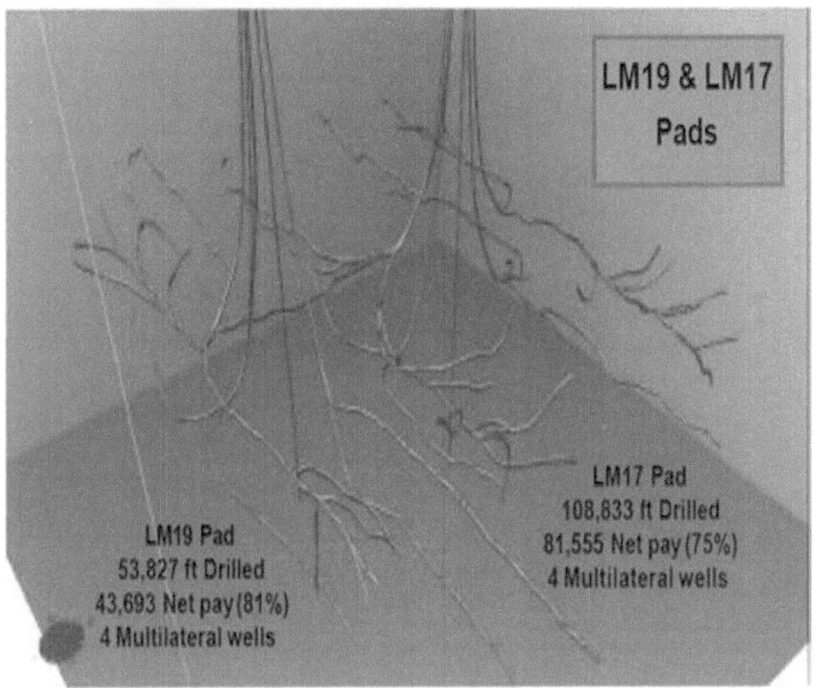

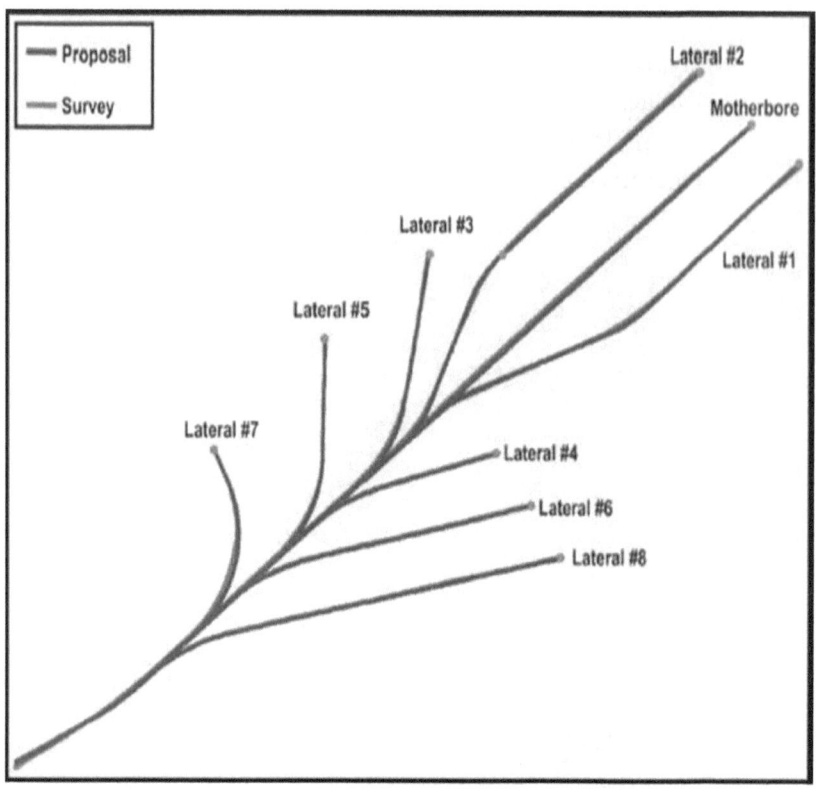

holes will be more beneficial than multi-fractured wells in developing tight gas fields.

Enyioha and Ertekin (2014) performed simulation study for advanced well structure model to forecast production performance of unconventional reservoirs.

Enyioha and Ertekin (2014) proposed a set of forward-acting and inverse-acting predictor models based on an artificial neural network framework and applied to advanced well structures in tight multi-phase systems. The forward-acting models forecast production rates, while the inverse-acting models generate well designs that can meet desired cumulative production profiles. Figure shows plots of oil rate, water rate, gas rate, and wellbore flowing pressure of fishbone well in numerical model and artificial neural network model. [1]

3.3.1. Shale gas well drilling

The first use of shale gas in the US can be traced back to 1821, when a shallow well drilled in the Devonian Dunkirk Shale in Chautauqua County, New York. The natural gas was produced, transported and sold to local establishments in the town of Fredonia. Following this discovery, hundreds of shallow shale wells were drilled along the Lake Erie shoreline and eventually several shale gas fields were established southeastward from the lake in the late 1800s. However, shale gas production had been discouraged because much larger volumes natural gas could produce from conventional reservoirs as with the Drake Well developed in 1859. These main stages in the shale gas industry from 1860 to 1970s were shale gas reservoirs discovered in the western Kentucky in 1863, in West Virginia in the

---

[1]Kun Sang Lee • Tae Hong Kim: Integrative Understanding of Shale Gas Reservoirs. 2016. P 118: 121

1920s, and hydraulic fracturing first used in the 1940s.

Time	Brief introduction
1821	In 1821, the first well was drilled in the Devonian Dunkirk Shale in Chautauqua County, New York. The natural gas was used to illuminate the town of Fredonia
1859	The Drake Well was developed in 1859 at Cherry tree Township, Venango County in the northwestern Pennsylvania. The Drake Well demonstrates that oil can be produced in large volumes. Hence, the Drake Well is viewed as one of the most important oil well ever drilled
1860s–1930s	(i) Shale-gas development spread westward along the southern shore of Lake Erie and reached northeastern Ohio in the 1870s. In 1863, gas was discovered in the western Kentucky part of the Illinois basin (ii) By the 1920s, drilling for shale gas had progressed into West Virginia, Kentucky, and Indiana (iii) By 1926, the Devonian shale gas fields of eastern Kentucky and West Virginia comprised the largest known gas occurrences in the world
Late 1940s	Hydraulic fracturing first used to stimulate oil and gas wells. The first hydraulic fracturing treatment was pumped in 1947 on a gas well operated by Pan American Petroleum Corporation in Grant County, Kansas

The 1973 and 1979 oil crises had led the U.S. to address energy shortages, and high price of oil. The oil crisis in 1970s propelled the U.S. government to invest in research and development and demonstration of alternative energy, including natural gas from shale formations. Meanwhile, the high oil prices attracted private enterprises to invest in unconventional natural gas.

Before 1970s, deep shale gas, such as the Barnett Shale in Texas and Marcellus in Pennsylvania, has been known but believed to have extremely low permeability and thus were not considered economically feasible. In the late

1970s, the U.S. Department of Energy (DOE) initiated the Eastern Gas Shale Project (EGSP) as a series of geological, geochemical, and petroleum engineering studies to evaluate the gas potential and to enhance gas production from the extensive Devonian and Mississippian organic-rich black shale within the Appalachian, Illinois, and Michigan basins in the eastern U.S.

In addition to providing R&D support, the Gas Research Institute (GRI) was established in 1977. The GRI was providing central organizations to manage the public research programs that were funded via mechanisms designed to pass research and development (R&D) costs through to the end-customer. A few years later, the DOE was established and funding for energy R&D, in general, and in particular, supplemental gas supplies, were substantially increased. During the 1980s and early 1990s, GRI was expanded to include R&D programs addressing supply, transmission, distribution and end-use. In the late 1990s, the National Energy Technology Laboratory (NETL) was established. A consolidated research program led by NETL was initiated aimed primarily at preventing pipeline damage of the aging natural gas infrastructure in the U.S. In the same time period, GRI was reorganized to emphasize near-term industry impact. In 2000, GRI and the Institute of Gas Technology (IGT), which had been the R&D performing laboratory for the gas distribution industry, merged to form the Gas Technology Institute (GTI).

Meanwhile, some pioneering oil and gas companies had tried to combine larger fracture designs, rigorous reservoir characterization, horizontal drilling, and lower cost approaches to hydraulic fracturing to make the extraction shale gas economic. The best-known pioneering company is the Mitchell Energy & Development Corp. The company went on to test various processes of hydraulic fracturing to exploit natural gas in the Barnett Shale formation in North Texas between 1981 and the early 1990s. Production from many of the 30 or so test wells fell short of covering operational costs. The company focused on the test results yielding the greatest returns. The engineers of this company analyzed and retested until eventually, the successful use of hydraulic fracturing to drill into shale formation for natural gas was completed. The hydraulic fracturing techniques developed by the Mitchell Energy & Development Corp. changed the face of the oil and gas industry

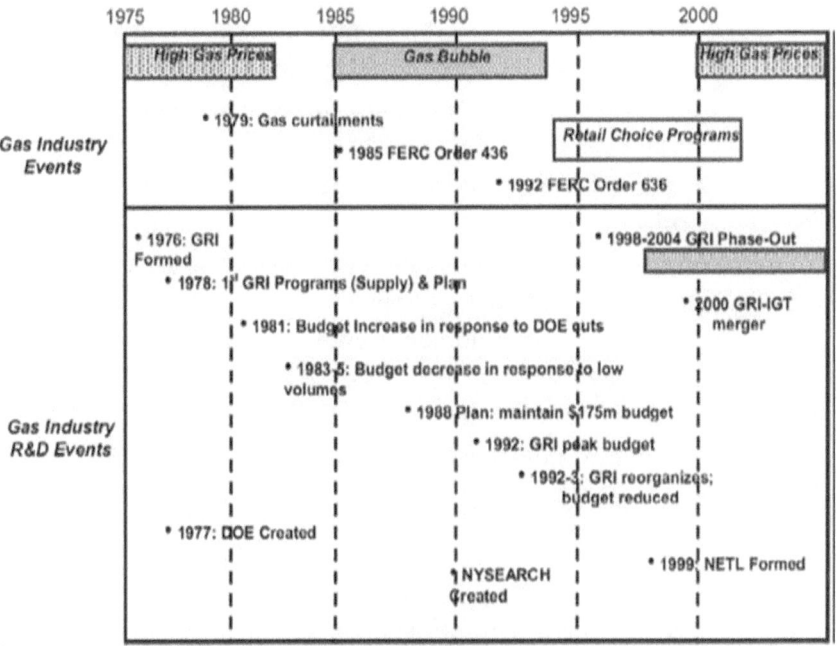

In a word, these efforts from government and private enterprise during this period contributed to the rapid growth in output of shale gas. The output of shale gas in the U.S. increased more than seven-fold between 1979 and 2000 (EIA 1999).

Since 2000, three factors have contributed to increase energy companies' confidence in the ability to profitably produce natural gas from the shale formation.

Above all, the drilling techniques are more advanced. In 2002, Devon Energy Corp. invested $3.5 billion in cash and stock to acquire

Mitchell Energy & Development Corp. Devon Energy Corp added horizontal drilling to its repertoire to make shale gas wells even more productive. In the few short years since then, technology has continued to improve: drilling techniques have continued to advance, and horizontal drilling has been employed by many exploration and production companies in search of unconventional resources. The use of horizontal drilling in conjunction with hydraulic fracturing greatly expanded the ability of producers to profitably produce natural gas from low permeability shale formations.

In addition, the rise in oil and gas prices since 2003 made shale gas more economically attractive than ever before. From the mid-1980s to 2003, the price of crude oil was generally under $25/barrel. The crude oil price rose above $30/barrel in 2003, reached $60/barrel in 2005, exceed $75/barrel in 2006, reached nearly $100/barrel in 2007, and peaked over $140/barrel in 2008. Finally, the prospect of falling conventional gas production of U.S. since 2000 triggered expectations of higher gas price inflation in. U.S. gas production was in slow but steady decline in the early 2000s. In the early 2000s, it was expected that U.S. natural gas

Economic study of Oil and Gas Well Drilling

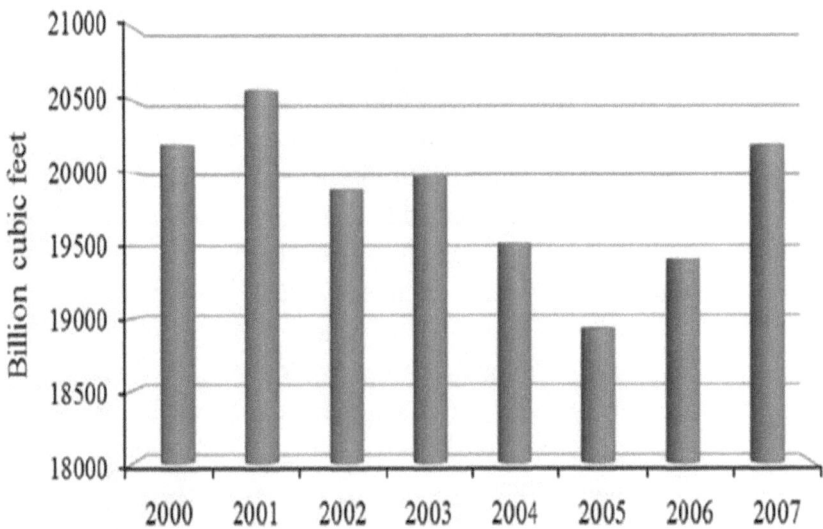

annual shale gas production
trillion cubic feet

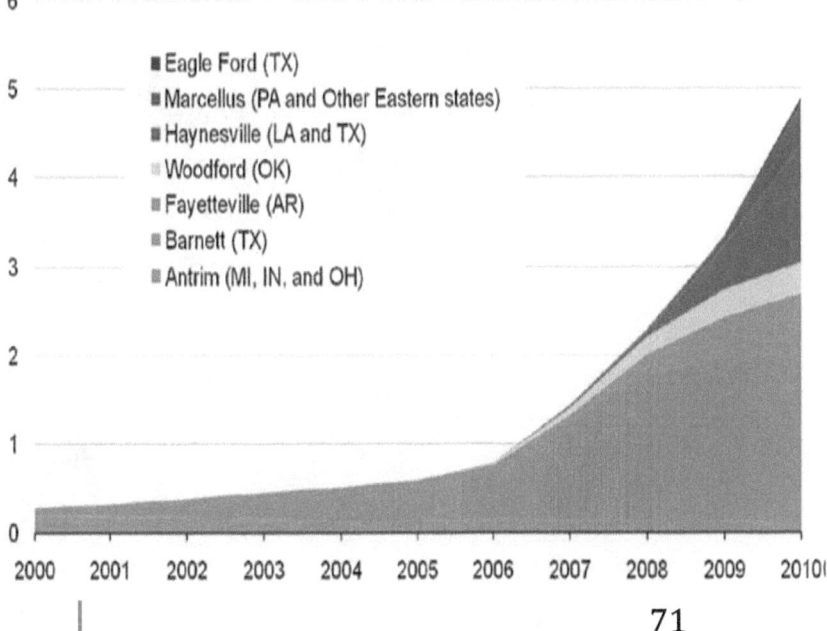

- Eagle Ford (TX)
- Marcellus (PA and Other Eastern states)
- Haynesville (LA and TX)
- Woodford (OK)
- Fayetteville (AR)
- Barnett (TX)
- Antrim (MI, IN, and OH)

price would rise in response to the resulting tight market.

Due to growing confidence in their ability to profitably produce natural gas in shale formations, the upstream oil and gas companies aggressively entered the shale gas business. Drilling for gas has increased sharply by the independent energy companies such as Devon Energy, Goodrich Petroleum, and XTO Energy. This can be shown by the development of the Barnett Shale Play, the largest producible reserves of any onshore natural gas field in the U.S. at that time

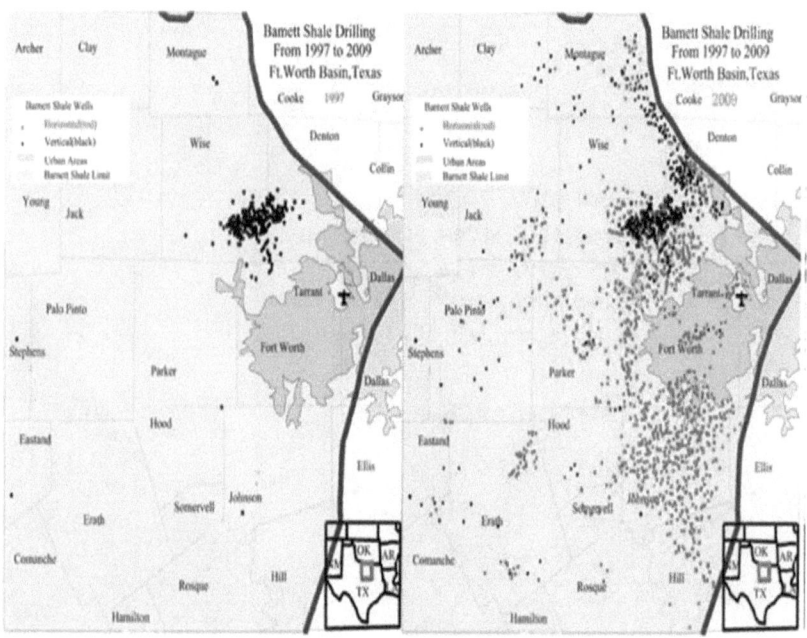

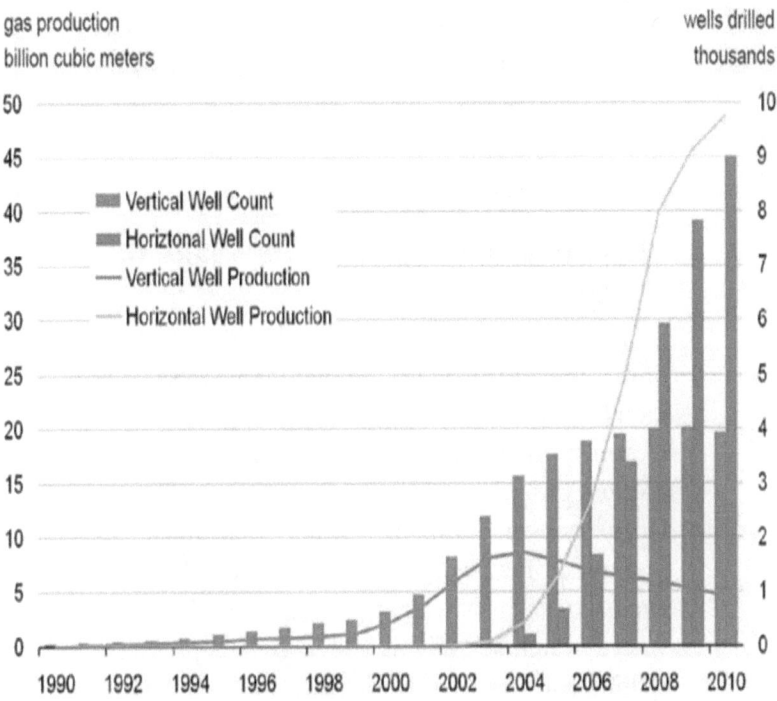

From 1997 to 2009, more than 13,500 gas wells have been drilled in the Barnett Shale Play. Naturally, the output of natural gas from the Barnett Shale Play increased sharply. In 2004, gas production from the Barnett Shale Play overtook the level of shallow shale gas production from historic shale plays such as the Appalachian Ohio Shale and Michigan Basin Antrim plays.

Inspired by the success of Barnett Shale Play, oil and gas companies rapidly entered other shale formation, including the Fayetteville Haynesville, Marcellus, Woodford,

Eagle Ford and other shale plays. The proliferation of activity in these new plays has increased shale gas production in the U.S. from 1.0 trillion cubic feet in 2006 to 4.87 trillion cubic feet, or 23 % of total U.S. natural gas production in 2010. [1]

3.3.2. Water Management in Shale Gas System

Water use is associated with each step of drilling and shale gas production process. It is known that the hydraulic fracturing operation requires millions of gallons of freshwater. In the Eagle Ford play of south Texas, for instance, large consumption of water resources in hydraulic fracturing would make the droughts even worse. In other regions, such as Marcellus where water scarcity is not a severe problem, spatial and seasonal variability in stream flow rates still raises the risk that water withdrawals may negatively impact water resources. Furthermore, as fracturing fluid is injected underground, a portion of water will flow back to the surface as highly contaminated water. The management of the flowback water and produced water is recognized as a greater challenge. [2]

---

[1]Kun Sang Lee • Tae Hong Kim: Integrative Understanding of Shale Gas Reservoirs. 2016. P 11: 16
[2]Georgios M. Kopanos · Pei Liu Michael C. Georgiadis: Advances in Energy Systems Engineering. Springer International Publishing Switzerland 2017. P 29

The wastewater generated in shale gas development typically contains the following compositions: dissolved salts, minerals, residual fracturing fluid additives, heavy metals, bacteria, suspended solids, naturally occurring radioactive material, volatile organics, hydrocarbons, and ammonia. In general, this water can be classified by the amount of total dissolved solids (TDS) per liter. Based on the operational definition, water produced during the well completion stage is defined as flowback water. On the other hand, water is referred to as produced water when the well is under production. Notably, the volumetric flow rate of flowback water is significantly larger than that of produced water, and the produced water tends to have higher concentration of TDS, likely because of its longer residence time downhole as well as smaller flow rate. As a whole, we can observe the flow rate of wastewater decreases along with time while the salinity of wastewater increases with time. The wastewater can be handled in multiple ways: direct injection into the Class II disposal wells, centralized wastewater treatment, and onsite treatment for reuse in hydraulic fracturing operations. [1]

---

[1] Georgios M. Kopanos · Pei Liu Michael C. Georgiadis: Advances in Energy Systems Engineering. Springer International Publishing Switzerland 2017. P 30

4. Primary production

Petroleum occurs in the microscopic pores of sedimentary rocks that form a reservoir – typically, reservoir rock consists of sand, sandstone, limestone, or dolomite. However, not all of the pores in a rock will contain petroleum – some will be filled with water or brine that is saturated with minerals. Both oil and gas have a low specific gravity relative to water and will thus float through the more porous sections of reservoir rock from their source area to the surface unless restrained by a trap. A trap is a reservoir that is overlain and underlain by dense impermeable cap rock or a zone of very low or no porosity that restrains migrating hydrocarbon. Reservoirs vary from being quite small to covering several thousands of acres, and range in thickness from a few inches to hundreds of feet or more.

In general, petroleum is extracted by drilling wells from an appropriate surface configuration into the hydrocarbon-bearing reservoir or reservoirs. Wells are designed to contain and control all fluid flow at all times throughout drilling and producing operations. The number of wells required is dependent on a combination of technical and economic factors used to determine the most likely range of recoverable reserves relative to a range of potential investment alternatives.

There are three phases for recovering oil from reservoirs: [1]

1. Primary recovery occurs as wells produce because of natural energy from expansion of gas and water within the producing formation, pushing fluids into the well bore and lifting the fluids to the surface.

2. Secondary recovery requires energy to be applied to lift fluids to surface – this may be accomplished by injecting gas down a hole to lift fluids to the surface, installation of a subsurface pump, or injecting gas or water into the formation itself.

3. Tertiary recovery occurs when a means is required to increase fluid mobility within the reservoir – this may be accomplished by introducing additional heat into the formation to lower the viscosity (thin the oil) and improve its ability to flow to the well bore. Heat may be introduced by either (1) injecting chemicals with water (chemical flood, surfactant flood), (2) injecting steam (steam flood), or (3) injecting oxygen to enable the ignition and combustion of oil within the reservoir (fire flood).

Production rates from reservoirs depend on a number of factors, such as reservoir

---

[1] Ripudaman Malhotra: Fossil Energy. Springer Science+Business Media New York 2013. P 26

geometry (primarily formation thickness and reservoir continuity), reservoir pressure, reservoir depth, rock type and permeability, fluid saturations and properties, extent of fracturing, number of wells and their locations, and the ratio of the permeability of the formation to the viscosity of the oil.

The geological variability of reservoirs means that production profiles differ from field to field. Heavy oil reservoirs can be developed to significant levels of production and maintained for a period of time by supplementing natural drive force, while gas reservoirs normally decline more rapidly. [1]

The primary production from a reservoir when the driving force is the expansion of oil plus the solution gas, will depend on the pressure being above or below the bubble point pb. As long as the reservoir pressure is above the bubble point, only oil is produced and the solution factor Rs of gas in the produced oil remains constant. When the pressure falls below the bubble point, the liberated gas may be produced into the wells together with the oil, and the produced gas to oil ratio (GOR) starts to increase. After some time, the driving force is exhausted and the production curve starts to fall. At the same time, water production (water cut)

---

[1] Ripudaman Malhotra: Fossil Energy. Springer Science+Business Media New York 2013. P 27

may start, which is unfavorable. The total recovery for such reservoirs is small (5–25 %). Preferentially, the gas should have remained in the reservoir to maintain the driving force. This can to some extent be achieved by a well strategy which allows the liberated gas to migrate away from the production wells to the top of the reservoir. [1]

In mediaeval days, oil was collected from seepages and even hand-dug wells, but before the nineteenth century had closed, drilling technology, which had already been developed for salt extraction, was adapted to the oil industry. The cable-tool, consisting of no more than a bullet-shaped weight on the end of a rope which thumped its way into the earth, was followed by the more efficient rotary rig, comprising a bit on the end of a rotating shaft, allowing the search to go deeper. Great technological progress was made in all aspects of the operation. [2]

While much early exploration was undertaken by the socalled wildcatters, drilling by guess and by God, it did not take long to discover the essential geological controls of

---

[1] Patrick A. Narbel • Jan Petter Hansen Jan R. Lien: Energy Technologies and Economics. Springer International Publishing Switzerland 2014. P 82

[2] C.J. Campbell: Campbell's Atlas of Oil and Gas Depletion. Colin J. Campbell and Alexander Wöstmann 2013. P 4

source, reservoir, trap and seal. At first, petroleum geologists relied on surface observations to identify promising prospects, endowed with the rare, right combination of circumstances, but before long they developed geophysical techniques to scan the depths. Both the technology and the interpretation became ever more sophisticated, assisted in more recent years by massive computing power. Perhaps the most important development of all was a geochemical breakthrough in the 1980s which elucidated the conditions for oil generation itself, making it possible to map accurately where oil was formed and where it was not. [1]

In technological terms, a major development was the semi-submersible rig, mounted on relatively stable pontoons beneath the wave-base, which opened up the continental shelves of the world to exploration, bringing in new production to replace the traditional onshore fields that were depleting. Even more elaborate floating production facilities later tapped the few Deepwater areas having the necessary geological conditions to yield oil.

The technical achievements of installing wellheads on the seabed and developing floating production facilities have been truly impressive. The operations are

---

[1] C.J. Campbell: Campbell's Atlas of Oil and Gas Depletion. Colin J. Campbell and Alexander Wöstmann 2013. P 4

constrained by the limit of the floating facilities, giving a plateau rather than a peak of production. Only large fields are commercially viable, given the high operating costs. Secondary recovery techniques, such as water-injection, are also constrained in the circumstances. It is even more difficult and expensive to produce deep water gas. Deepwater operations test technology to the limit and there have been occasional accidents, including the serious Macondo accident in the Gulf of Mexico in 2010, when 11 men lost their lives and widespread pollution had a serious economic and environmental impact on the US coastline. [1]

The move to the deep water heralded another wave of optimism, as economists, looking at their office atlas, concluded that there were vast oceans about to deliver a limitless new supply of oil, but again the geological constraints began to manifest themselves, as it became evident that very special combination of geological circumstances had to be met.

The deep water finds off South America, Africa and in the Gulf of Mexico rely on oil generated in the rifts that opened as the continents began to move apart, 150 million years ago.

---

[1] C.J. Campbell: Campbell's Atlas of Oil and Gas Depletion. Colin J. Campbell and Alexander Wöstmann 2013. P 371

At first, the rifts were filled with fresh water to become lakes, resembling those of East Africa today, but then the sea broke in. It was subject to a high level of evaporation under the warm climate of the time, which led to the deposition of a thick layer of salt, which sealed the underlying oil. Later, about 60 million years ago, sands and clays, which had been deposited at the mouths of rivers on the adjoining continents, slumped down the continental slope. In some areas they were then taken back into suspension by ocean currents which winnowed out the fi ne-grained material depositing pods of porous sand on the ocean floor. Still later, structural movements locally ruptured the salt seal to allow the oil to migrate upwards and collect the pods of sandstone, which formed excellent reservoirs for oil. The remarkable combination of circumstances is obvious. Successful attempts are now being made to penetrate the salt seal itself and find what is left beneath it, with some promising results in Brazil, albeit at a depth of about 5,000 m. [1]

The leases have been acquired. The geologic and geophysical data have been interpreted, maps have been made, depth to the objective pay zone has been calculated, and a location has been staked. Now the acid test is begun. The well is spudded in. No one knows if

---

[1] C.J. Campbell: Campbell's Atlas of Oil and Gas Depletion. Colin J. Campbell and Alexander Wöstmann 2013. P 371: 372

you have hydrocarbons until you get there, until you get to the pay zone, until you get to the proposed depth.

Far in advance of the day that the well is spudded in, the drilling engineers prepare a drilling plan. The questions they must answer or be prepared to answer as drilling progresses are many: What sizes and types of bits will they use? How deep will they set the surface casing? Will they set intermediate strings, and if so, where will they set them? What kind of drilling mud will they use, and how should it be weighted to counteract the pressure they expect to encounter? Where do they expect to find production? When will they log, and what suite of logs will be run? When will they make drill stem tests? As the well is drilled, they must be prepared to modify their plan in accordance with what they encounter. If it is a wildcat well, they may be in for some real surprises. If it is a development well, the chances are that the drilling program will be fairly routine. [1]

Because of the risk involved and the possibility of great gain, oil exploration is often considered a gamble, a hit or miss proposition. But its real nature is closer to hunting than gambling. There is a difference. Gambling matches skill against luck; hunting matches skill

---

[1] R.L.Sengbush: petroleum exploration, a quantitative introduction, library of congress 1st edition 1986. p 67

against luck and nature. The part of nature that interests the petroleum explorationist is the earth's crust, which has been deformed and twisted, uplifted and eroded, in no regular pattern of assault through the geologic ages. The crust has become a puzzle, and within the puzzle lies the quarry, hydrocarbons-oil and gas-trapped on anticlines, or at faults or salt domes or truncations or pinch outs or reefs. The foremost weapons of the hunt are the ability to gather information about the earth's strata in the present state, and then the ability to imagine how the strata arrived at this state through the geologic ages. [1]

Hydrocarbons are not hunted with drilling rigs; the rigs confirm or deny the work of intelligence and imagination that went before. A rotary drilling rig simply rotates into the earth a hollow steel pipe on the bottom of which is a bit, and the rotation and weight of the drill string on the bit chisels out a hole. The cuttings from the bottom are lifted out of the hole by the drilling mud that is pumped down the pipe, out through holes in the bit, and back up to the surface in the annulus between the pipe and the hole. The drilling mud also cools the bit, conditions the hole by keeping the shales from sloughing off into the hole and causing the pipe to stick and prevents damage to productive

---

[1] R.L.Sengbush: petroleum exploration, a quantitative introduction, library of congress 1st edition 1986. p 68

formations and controls pressure A drilling rig digs a hole and carries the cuttings out.

A drilling rig provides power through huge engines to rotate the bit, circulate the mud, and hoist the pipe in and out of the hole. The rig is under direct control of a driller who operates the draw works and keeps an eye on the weight indicator, which tells him the weight of the drill string on the bit. The "roughnecks" grab up a stem of pipe with tongs, and the "derrick man," sitting high above the derrick floor works the end of the pipe into place. [1]

Over recent decades new drilling technologies has been developed and implemented, resulting in a dramatic increase in U.S. natural gas production: "hydraulic fracturing" and "horizontal drilling." In hydraulic fracturing, the older of the two techniques, an energy production firm drills a well into a reservoir containing gas or oil and carefully seals the well bore so that it can withstand pressurization. The driller then forces a combination of water, sand, and a mixture of chemicals through the well and into the surrounding rock. The pressure fractures the friable rock, allowing gas to percolate into the well and up to the well's collection point.

---

[1] R.L.Sengbush: petroleum exploration, a quantitative introduction, library of congress 1st edition 1986. P 68

More recently, U.S. firms have succeeded in drilling horizontally through shale beds to reach more gas from a single surface well. In this process the driller sinks a vertical well, which may be a mile deep, to reach a gas-containing shale bed. At this point, the exploration company turns the drill sideways and continues to drill horizontally through the shale rock. When drilling stops, the driller removes the drill and introduces small holes into the well casing surrounded by the shale by igniting controlled explosions. With the holes in the well casing in place, the driller pumps fracturing fluid, a mix of water, sand, and chemicals, into the horizontal portion of the well, causing the shale bed to fracture and release gas back into the well. This process of horizontal drilling and hydraulic fracturing can be repeated from a single vertical well, thereby reducing the number of vertical wells required to exploit a gas field and reducing the drilling footprint at the earth's surface.

In the United States, natural gas produced by unconventional methods already exceeds that produced by older conventional methods, and the U.S. Energy Information Administration predicts that by 2035, unconventional gas will constitute fully 75 % of U.S. production. In the last three decades, U. S. natural gas production has increased by 50 % and reserves have almost doubled due largely to the advent of shale gas. Most strikingly, the U.S.

Energy Information Administration notes that shale gas production surged from 0.39 trillion cubic feet in 2000 to 4.87 trillion cubic feet in 2010, jumping by a factor of more than twelve times in a single decade. The changing supply and production levels have had profound consequences for prices. After peaking in 2008, prices for natural gas fell by 80 % and have recovered to less than 40 % of the 2008 maximum. Over this period, the price of crude oil has remained high, so the cost per unit of energy in the form of natural gas has become quite inexpensive compared to that of oil.

While the natural gas revolution has thus far been primarily a U.S. development, other nations are changing that very rapidly, as many other nations possess their own shale gas resources. In an initial assessment, the U.S. Energy Information Administration concluded that "...the international shale gas resource base is vast," even though the report assessed only 32 countries outside the U.S. and excluded Russia, Central Asia, the Middle East, South East Asia and Central Africa from the analysis. The study found tremendous resources in every continent except Antarctica, with apparently very large deposits in Canada, South America, South Africa, the Maghreb, Europe, China, and Australia. Very active efforts are underway in many of these areas to develop the necessary technology and to exploit these newly discovered gas reserves. For instance, China has actively been acquiring some U.S. firms with hydraulic fracturing and horizontal drilling expertise and has been partnering with other such firms.

Beyond the techniques of hydraulic fracturing and horizontal drilling, a third critical element that features in the natural gas revolution is the build-out of the LNG (liquid natural gas) infrastructure and market. Natural gas can move from a gas field to elsewhere in three main ways: via pipeline, via compression and transport by rail or truck, or via liquefaction and transport by ship. Of these three, pipeline transmission is cheapest in the normal event. Compression is not scalable, because compressing reduces the volume of natural gas by a factor of only about 100, leaving road or rail transport prohibitively expensive. LNG technology is not new, but the rapid development of an ever-expanding LNG infrastructure constitutes an important part of the story of natural gas. Liquefaction reduces the volume of natural gas by a factor of 600, allowing transport by ship.

Building pipelines from natural gas fields to markets is ruinously expensive, and most pipeline developments can proceed only with an assured market for the natural gas. Thus, pipeline contracts have typically called for gas purchasers to enter long term contracts for natural gas with gas prices linked to oil. With current low natural gas prices, the contract price for many of these pipeline-delivered supplies costs five to eight times as much as the current spot price of natural gas in world markets.

Because so much of the world's natural gas production and delivery system has been governed by these pipeline contracts, a world market for natural gas has been slow to develop. That is now rapidly changing with enormous implications. Three countries illustrate the power of these developments. Qatar has very rich gas resources, but with its location in the Persian Gulf, it is a long way from markets.

However, it has become a very robust LNG supplier, with immediate access through the Straits of Hormuz to the open sea. For its part, Japan almost totally lacks hydrocarbon deposits. In the wake of the March 2011 Fukushima nuclear disaster Japan shuttered its nuclear plants, making it ever more dependent on the delivery of overseas oil and natural gas. For its part, Australia now suddenly appears to be poised to be a major LNG supplier, further enriching the world supply of gas and strengthening the movement toward a genuinely world market.

The price of LNG by long-term contract has typically been much greater than the spot market price of gas. Part of this differential can be attributed to the higher cost of LNG delivery. To liquefy gas requires a very expensive liquefaction plant that can chill the gas to its liquefaction point of -260 F. Then the liquefied gas must be transported by ship, which costs considerably more than pipeline transmission.

However, much of the excess cost of LNG over the spot market price exceeds the actual cost of liquefaction and delivery. With a burgeoning LNG infrastructure and a number of new suppliers in the market, one can reasonably expect the price of LNG-delivered gas to fall toward the spot market price plus the added cost of liquefaction and transport. This will be an enormous benefit to countries such as Japan.

Further, the development of a robust LNG market gives many nations a choice of using LNG or pipeline-delivered gas. For example, India has an extensive coastline and can receive LNG quite readily. If gas must be delivered by pipeline over a very long distance, over very rugged terrain, and across many national boundaries, with each transit country imposing a fee, the price differential between LNG and pipeline gas can be seriously eroded or even erased. Thus, the natural gas revolution holds out the promise to radically expand worldwide supplies, to allow many nations to develop domestic resources that were previously thought inaccessible, and to facilitate a worldwide market in natural gas through an improved and elaborated LNG infrastructure.

However, potentially devastating environmental consequences associated with the technique of hydraulic fracturing lie at the heart of the natural gas revolution.

First, the chemicals used in the fracturing fluid might leak into aquifers and cause serious water contamination. Second, hydraulic fracturing might cause earthquakes, and there is some evidence that this has occurred already. Third, hydraulic fracturing requires water, usually 2–4 million gallons per well. Clearly, using water for gas-drilling competes with other potential uses. However, hydraulic fracturing advocates point out that even in very dry climes, the fraction of water devoted to gas drilling is really quite small. Fourth, natural gas drilling creates disruption at the surface, including scarring of the land, unsightly drilling rigs, and the introduction of heavy vehicle traffic into rural areas. In addition, when the drillers enter a region the riches it brings to some, but only some, local residents, may alter the culture of areas that suddenly become targets of a gas boom. With so much at stake—wealth, access to energy, the future of the world's energy mix, and the environment, including the entire question of hydrocarbons and global climate change—much of the environmental debate surrounding hydraulic fracturing has become highly politicized with heavy sparring and self-serving analyses being offered by both industry lobbying interests and environmental pressure groups. [1]

From the very beginning of the drilling, the mud returns are analyzed by mud loggers. They observe the cuttings that are coming from the bottom and record the geologic information about the type of rocks being cut, the percentage of sand, and other interesting geologic properties. They also record the drilling rate because the drilling rate depends on the type of formation that one is drilling in and the condition of the bit. They also observe the mud for indications of hydrocarbons. The mud loggers are often the first persons to detect the presence of hydrocarbons at depth. The detection is usually by means of fluorescence. This is the mud logger's job, to record the geologic and physical properties of the cuttings, record the drilling rate, and look for fluorescence. [2]

Now suppose the loggers observe a possible zone of hydrocarbons. Then the drilling engineer will make a decision whether or not to log the hole, and if so, will select the suite of logs to be run. Suppose the logs are run and a

---

[1] Andre' Dorsman • Timur Go"k • Mehmet Baha Karan: Perspectives on Energy Risk. Springer-Verlag Berlin Heidelberg 2014. P 73: 76
[2] R.L.Sengbush: petroleum exploration, a quantitative introduction, library of congress 1st edition 1986. p 68

good possibility of economic hydrocarbons is indicated. Then a decision is made

whether or not to make a drill stem test. If a test is decided on, the tool will be set at the level at which hydrocarbons have been detected on the logs, packers will be set on each side of the tool to keep contamination out. The pressure in the zone of interest will be lowered, allowing the well to flow under controlled conditions. The test results will give an indication of the pressure and the fluid content in the formation Now suppose the test indicates a possible discovery of hydrocarbons, but the well has not reached the objective depth. Then a decision must be made to stop here and try to produce these hydrocarbons, or to drill deeper.

Suppose the engineers decide to drill deeper and do not want to destroy the hydrocarbon potential of the zone just tested. Then after setting an intermediate string of casing through the potential zone, the cement trucks will be called again and an intermediate casing will be set to protect the potential hydrocarbon zone. After the cement is set up, the cement plug will be drilled out and drilling continued. [1]

---

[1] R.L.Sengbush: petroleum exploration, a quantitative introduction, library of congress 1st edition 1986. P 70

At objective depth, the loggers will be called in again to run a suite of logs. If the logs indicate that the objective zone has hydrocarbons, a drill stem test will be made. If this zone looks economic, a third set of casing, called a production string, will be set with cement. Now two potential horizons sit behind casing. To produce the deeper horizon and to save the shallower horizon for later, the casing is perforated by shooting charges through the casing at the level of the producing zone, and production then will be made through the perforations that have been made in the production string. [1]

Every oil well drilling rig must be equipped with systems that enable the rig to meet seven separate but interrelated requirements: [2]

1. Penetrate the subsurface strata.

2. Excavate the drill cuttings.

3. Prevent the caving of penetrated strata.

4. Penetrate deep enough to reach the target reservoir.

---

[1] R.L.Sengbush: petroleum exploration, a quantitative introduction, library of congress 1st edition 1986. p 70
[2] Ellis H.Austin: Drilling Engineering, International Human Resources Development Corporation • Boston D. Reidel Publishing Company, 1983. P 1

5. Drill a hole large enough for efficient production of the reservoir fluids.

6. Keep the hole oriented in the desired direction.

7. Prevent the intrusive fluids from entering the hole.

In modern drilling rigs this is achieved by means of four separate systems: [1]

1. a power plant and transmission system;

2. a hoisting system;

3. a rotating system; and

4. a circulating system.

4.1. Power Plant and Transmission System

On most modern drilling rigs the power is supplied by gas or diesel engines or by a diesel-electric system. **In** direct-drive gas or diesel engines, the power is transmitted to other systems through clutches to a compound which, in turn, is connected by chain drives or by fluid couplings with torque converters. Pumps are usually driven by belt drives.

---

[1]Ellis H.Austin: Drilling Engineering, International Human Resources Development Corporation • Boston D. Reidel Publishing Company, 1983. P 1

Shallow- or moderate-depth rigs (to 5,000 ft or so) require from 500 to 1,000 hp, whereas, heavy-duty rigs require up to 3,000 hp or more. An additional power plant of 100 to 500 hp often provides auxiliary power for lighting, mixing equipment, logging units, etc.

4.2. Hoisting Equipment

The hoisting system is used primarily to raise and lower the drill pipe in the hole and to maintain the desired weight on the bottom. This system is designed to handle various weights up to some 500,000 pounds or more of dead weight on the hook, depending upon the depth capabilities of the rig, Derrick load capacities vary from 250,000 to 1,500,000 pounds and can stand wind loading from 100 to 130 miles per hours. [1]

4.3. Rotating Equipment

The rotating equipment is used solely to provide a rotating motion to the drill bit at the bottom of the hole. The system includes the rotary swivel, the kelly, the rotary table and Kelly bushing, the drill pipe and drill collars, and the drill bit. [2]

---

[1] Ellis H.Austin: Drilling Engineering, International Human Resources Development Corporation • Boston D. Reidel Publishing Company, 1983. P 2: 5

[2] Ellis H.Austin: Drilling Engineering, International Human Resources Development Corporation • Boston D. Reidel Publishing Company, 1983. P 5

Rotary drill bits are essentially all of a similar design; that is, they have three freely rotating cones which bear on the rock and do the actual drilling. The cones are of two basic types, with either milled teeth or with tungsten carbide inserts, which break and remove the rock by intrusion, pressure breaking, and dragging. Toothed bits are normally used to **drill** soft to moderately hard formations, while insert bits are used on moderately hard to very hard abrasive formations, with considerable overlapping and a current trend toward a more widespread use of insert bits.

For extremely hard formations and for some coring operations, coneless bits with industrial diamond inserts are used. Although quite expensive, such bits are often capable of considerably more drilled footage than insert-type core bits. [1]

4.4. Circulating System

The drilling fluid, or mud, makes a circuit through the circulating system of the drilling rig, Mud is mixed at the mixing hopper from the base fluid, usually water, and the bulk materials in the mud house. From there, it goes to the suction pit, where it is picked up by the mud pumps to begin its circuit. It travels up the

---

[1]Ellis H.Austin: Drilling Engineering, International Human Resources Development Corporation • Boston D. Reidel Publishing Company, 1983. P 8

stand pipe, through the kelly hose (rotary hose or mud hose) and enters the drill column through the swivel. In the drill column, it travels downward through the kelly cock, kelly, drill pipe, drill collars, and water courses of the bit into the drilled hole. There, it picks up drill cuttings and travels with them up the drilled annulus through the blowout preventers and mud return line to the shale shaker. There, the larger cuttings are screened out, and the mud flows into a settling pit from where it returns through the sump pit to the suction pit to begin the circuit once again. [1]

From the shale shaker, the cutting and contaminated mud are diverted to a so-called reserve pit, which is actually a waste pit rather than a true reserve supply. On most modern rigs, the suction, settling, and sump pits are actually steel tanks rather than the dirt pits of a few years ago. [2]

There are two types of auxiliary systems associated with the basic circulating system, the equipment necessary for well pressure control. The former includes mud pit agitators for maintenance of a uniform content of mud solids, cone-type desanders and desilters

---

[1] Ellis H.Austin: Drilling Engineering, International Human Resources Development Corporation • Boston D. Reidel Publishing Company, 1983. P 8: 10
[2] Ellis H.Austin: Drilling Engineering, International Human Resources Development Corporation • Boston D. Reidel Publishing Company, 1983. P 11

to remove contaminants that would not settle out otherwise, and a vacuum degaser for removal of entrained gases. [1]

---

[1] Ellis H.Austin: Drilling Engineering, International Human Resources Development Corporation • Boston D. Reidel Publishing Company, 1983. P 11

5. Drilling Fluids

Although the drilling of a well is a complex operation involving many different mechanical elements and processes, the single most important factor upon which the successful completion of the well depends is the drilling-fluid circulation system. The majority of serious problems encountered during drilling, including lost circulation, stuck pipe, kicking wells, poor penetration performance, high costs, blowouts, and poor-quality well logs, can all be traced back to poorly designed, misunderstood, and misused drilling-fluid systems.

The primary functions of the drilling fluid and its circulation systems are: [1]

1. To remove rock cuttings from the bottom of the hole so that the bit can drill on a fresh rock surface, thereby increasing the efficiency of the drilling operation.

2. To transport the cuttings to the surface where they can be removed from the drilling fluid.

3. To suspend the cuttings in the hole whenever mud circulation is stopped.

4. To cool and lubricate the bit and clean its cutting surface.

---

[1] Ellis H.Austin: Drilling Engineering, International Human Resources Development Corporation • Boston D. Reidel Publishing Company, 1983. P 32: 33

5. To exert sufficient hydrostatic pressure to exclude formation fluids from the hole.

6. To maintain a stable, lubricated well bore that can be reentered at any time during the drilling operation.

Of secondary importance, but critical to reservoir evaluation and control, is the requirement that the drilling should be conducive to obtaining reliable logs of good quality and should have filtration properties to prevent contamination of productive strata. By the same token, it should not deposit a mud cake so thick as to reduce the hole diameter to the point of creating a swabbing action as the drill pipe is reciprocated or causing the pipe to stick. [1]

5.1. Oil-Base Muds

Drilling fluids that contain oil as the continuous liquid phase are called *oil-base* or *oil muds*. Such muds always contain some water, and if the water is emulsified as a useful constituent, the mud is called an *invert-emulsion mud*. [2]

---

[1] Ellis H.Austin: Drilling Engineering, International Human Resources Development Corporation • Boston D. Reidel Publishing Company, 1983. P 33

[2] Ellis H.Austin: Drilling Engineering, International Human Resources Development Corporation • Boston D. Reidel Publishing Company, 1983. P 41

Principal applications for oil muds are: (1) to prevent damage to the productive formation by the drilling fluid; (2) to drill or core evaporites; (3) to drill troublesome shales; (4) to overcome wall sticking of drill pipe; (5) to release stuck pipe; (6) to drill under extreme temperature conditions, high temperatures in very deep holes and low temperatures in permafrost and cold climates; (7) to place in the tubing-casing annulus and the casing-hole annulus to facilitate recovery of pipe; and (8) to drill formations containing corrosive fluids, such as hydrogen sulfide.

Oil makes up 60 to 98% of the liquids in oil muds. Diesel fuel is commonly used, although some crude oils are satisfactory. For reasons of safety, the flash point of the oil should be above 160°F. The analine point should be at least 150°F to minimize damage to rubber parts. Oil-resistant rubber should be used wherever rubber parts come in contact with oil mud. Winter-grade diesel oil is required in extremely cold weather. [1]

Water, the dispersed or emulsified phase, is present in amounts of 2 to 40% by volume. Between 15 and 30% is normal for invert-emulsion muds. Water from almost any source is acceptable (an exception is produced

---

[1] Ellis H.Austin: Drilling Engineering, International Human Resources Development Corporation • Boston D. Reidel Publishing Company, 1983. P 41: 42

water that contains emulsion breakers) because the chemical composition of the water usually is adjusted for the particular application of the oil mud. For example, calcium chloride is added to the water to improve the hole stability in shale.

The other components of oil muds are varied. Often the oil mud is mixed at a central mixing plant and delivered to the well site where barite is added if needed. Although the composition differs among the several commercial oil muds, the constituents serve to provide the properties necessary for: (1) suspension, such as organophilic clays, asphalt; (2) emulsification, such as calcium soaps, may be formed in the system by reaction of quick lime and fatty acids; (3) filtration, such as asphalt, resins, lignite derivative; (4) oil wetting, such as lecithin; (5) shale stabilization, such as calcium chloride, salt; (6) viscosity reduction, such as petroleum sulfonates; and (7) increase density, such as limestone, barite. [1]

5.2. Shale Stabilization by Oil Mud

An obvious solution to hole problems arising from the absorption of water by shales would appear to be the use of a drilling fluid that has oil as the liquid phase. Experience has shown, however, that oil muds always contain

---

[1] Ellis H. Austin: Drilling Engineering, International Human Resources Development Corporation • Boston D. Reidel Publishing Company, 1983. P 42

some water and that the hole stability sometimes is affected. Laboratory studies show that wet shales can be hardened by exposure to invert-emulsion mud that contains a high-salinity water in the emulsified phase.

Two methods have been used to estimate the salinity required. The first method (Mondshine) equates the surface hydration force of shale with the matrix stress (equal to the overburden pressure minus the pore fluid pressure). The salinity of the interstitial water is measured or estimated, and the required salinity is read from a graph. The other method (Chenevert) involves the measurement of the equilibrium vapor pressure of the shale (from cuttings) and adjustment of salinity of the emulsified water to the same or somewhat lower vapor pressure. As a practical field approach, the salinity of the water in the oil mud is raised to a concentration substantially above that estimated for the water in the shale. Maintaining a stable emulsion takes advantage of osmotic forces across the semipermeable membrane to transfer water from the shale into the drilling fluid. In this way, the borehole wall may be made stronger. [1]

---

[1] Ellis H.Austin: Drilling Engineering, International Human Resources Development Corporation • Boston D. Reidel Publishing Company, 1983. P 43

5.3. Gas (Air) Drilling Fluid

The term *reduced-pressure drilling* has been applied to drilling with a circulating medium with a density less than that of water. This class of drilling fluids ranges from dry gas through mist, foam, "stiff foam", to aerated mud.

The principal benefit derived from air and aerated drilling fluids is the gain in penetration rate resulting from the lowered differential pressure. Weak formations can be drilled without loss of circulation. Producing formations are not damaged by invasion of the drilling fluid. Problems arise with dry-air drilling water bearing strata are penetrated. Cuttings stick to the wet borehole and may plug the annulus. After a water-producing formation has been entered, the amount of water coming into the hole will control the drilling rate. If water-sensitive formations are exposed, hole problems will develop. Often the difficulties involved in "mudding-up" an air-drilled hole offset the savings made during that period of fast drilling. [1]

5.4. Application of Nitrogen

During drilling operation when loss circulation occurs, especially when a light-weight mud is used, nitrogen can be injected into

---

[1]Ellis H.Austin: Drilling Engineering, International Human Resources Development Corporation • Boston D. Reidel Publishing Company, 1983. P 44: 45

the mud system at the standpipe to lower hydrostatic pressure on bottom.

Nitrogen has the advantages over other aerated systems because pressure, volume, and temperature can be controlled to a great degree of accuracy. Temperature could be one of the factors to be considered while working with an aerated system. Assuming that 300,000 scf of nitrogen would be required over a period of time to control hydrostatic pressure at depth and that the gas was to be pumped into the mud system at ambient temperature, whereas the wellbore temperature was 130 of, we have a new volume factor: [1]

$$V_2 = V_1 \times \frac{T_2}{T_1} = 300,000 + 15 \frac{130 + 460}{70 + 460} = 33,916 \text{ scf.}$$

At greater well bore temperatures, the volume increases proportionally and can result in unloading the annulus. Tables developed by suppliers are designed for a geothermal gradient of 1.6 of per 100 ft of depth.

The nitrogen line is connected to the standpipe during drilling operations and nitrogen is pumped at the required rate until the kelly joint is down. Before breaking the kelly joint, the nitrogen pumping is discounted and a safety

---

[1] Ellis H.Austin: Drilling Engineering, International Human Resources Development Corporation • Boston D. Reidel Publishing Company, 1983. P 47: 48

mud cap is pumped to simulate a depth of approximately 1000 ft in the drill pipe to prevent unloading. Low solubility of nitrogen in the mud system gives ample time to make up a joint before nitrogen works its way back to the surface. A heavy mud in the 14-lb range may reduce the amount of safety mud cap required to make up a new joint.

Often during drilling operations, a lost circulation zone is encountered at shallow to medium depths, while a high-pressure zone is being drilled at a much lower depth. In this type situation, nitrogen can be injected into the mud system again at the standpipe to lower the hydrostatic pressure at shallow depths, while at the same time maintaining a safe overburden at the greater depths. [1]

was encountered at 6249 ft. The entire lost circulation material amounted to 25 lb/bbl, giving a mud weight of 8.4 lb and a 35-second viscosity, yet 750 bbl were lost to the formation and returns ceased. In an attempt to drill the additional 50 to 100 ft necessary to complete the well, the drill pipe got stuck. [2]

---

[1]Ellis H.Austin: Drilling Engineering, International Human Resources Development Corporation • Boston D. Reidel Publishing Company, 1983. P 48
[2]Ellis H.Austin: Drilling Engineering, International Human Resources Development Corporation • Boston D. Reidel Publishing Company, 1983. P 49

It was confirmed that the pipe stuck at 5287 ft due to formation caving, with no differential sticking above the caving zone. Drilling mud was retreated with no circulation material lost, viscosity increased to 45 seconds and a loss of 12 cc of water. A thousand feet of drill pipe and the 61;.1" drill collars were to be recovered by wash over, and fishing without assurance of circulation could increase the risk that the 7%" 0 D wash pipe would get stuck in the same manner as the original one. The nitrogen pumps used in Oklahoma had a minimum stroke of 200 scf/min, whereby the maximum practical mud-pump stroke during the wash over was 4 to 6 BPM. Gas concentration thus ranged from 30 to 50 scf/ bbl, resulting in an apparent nitrified density of 7 lb/gal from the nonaerated 8.4 lb/gal and in lowering the hydrostatic pressure at 6253 ft from 2726 psi, which adequately maintained stability at the weak zone. A lower gas concentration would have been satisfactory could the two systems (nitrogen pumps and mud pumps) have been adjusted to lower the gas-pump rate. A total of 294,000 scf was used during the five-day fishing job, drilling 42 ft of hole, and conditioning for casing and logging. [1]

---

[1] Ellis H.Austin: Drilling Engineering, International Human Resources Development Corporation • Boston D. Reidel Publishing Company, 1983. P 49: 50

6. Fracking Technology

The gas bearing stratum of tight shale, typically about 3 km below the surface and 20–150m in thickness, is accessed by parallel horizontal boreholes, about 500m apart. They are drilled from a single drill pad in the direction of the minimum principal tectonic stress σh, whose magnitude is about 1/5 to 4/5 of the overburden stress σg.

The horizontal boreholes used to be about 3 km long, but 11 km is now being attained. Each of them is subdivided into segments about 600m long, each of which consists of about 5–10 fracturing stages. Each stage, typically 70m long, is further subdivided into about 5–8 perforation clusters. In each cluster, about 14m long, the steel casing (or pipe), of typical inner diameter 3.5 in. (77 mm), is perforated at 5–8 locations by detonating groups of shaped explosive charges.

Powerful pumps on the surface drill pad inject the fracking fluid into the shale stratum. The fluid, about 99% water, contains proppant (a fine sand needed to prevent crack closure), and contains various additives, particularly gellants, various acids or pH controlling ions. Each stage requires injection of several million gallons of water (which is equivalent to about 0.5–2mm of rain over the area of the lease, 3 * 5 to 10km^2). The flowback of water, representing about 15% of the injected total, is very salty and highly contaminated with dissolved minerals. Strict controls are required to prevent its accidental release to the environment. Often, the water

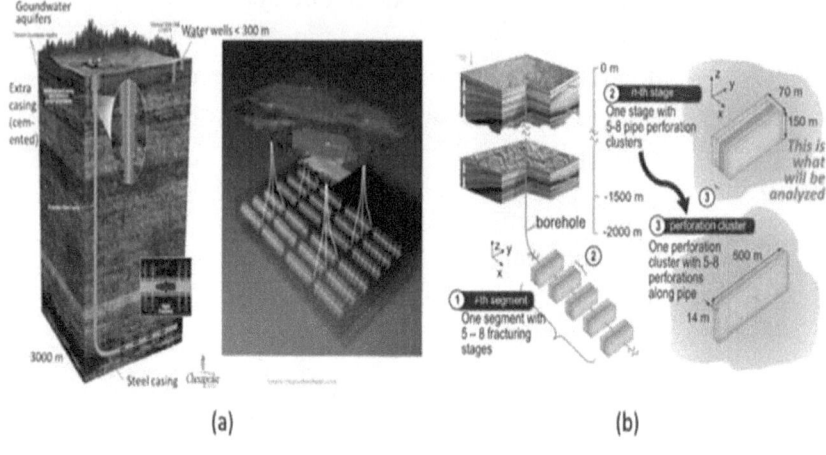

(a) (b)

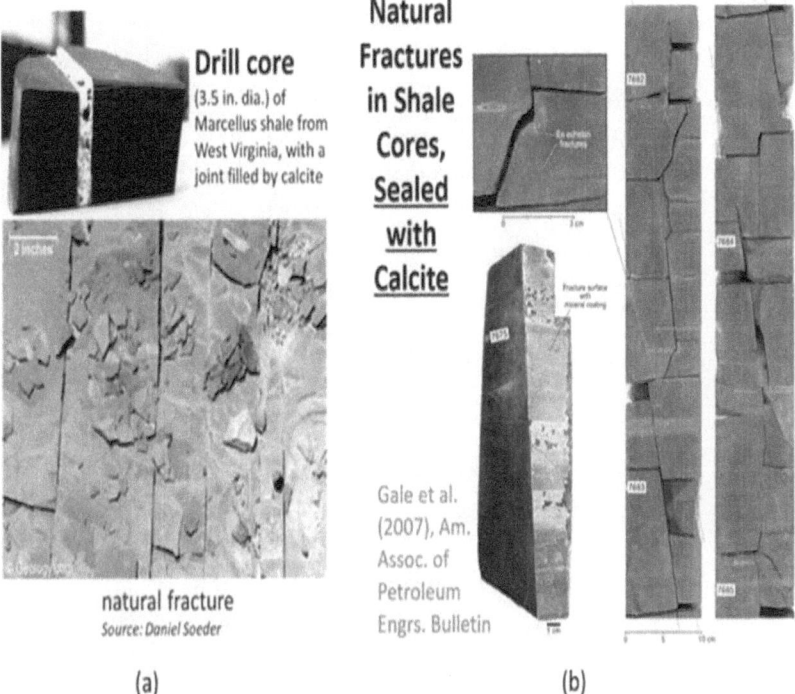

(a) Drill core (3.5 in. dia.) of Marcellus shale from West Virginia, with a joint filled by calcite; natural fracture. Source: Daniel Soeder

(b) Natural Fractures in Shale Cores, Sealed with Calcite. Gale et al. (2007), Am. Assoc. of Petroleum Engrs. Bulletin

flowback is reinjected underground. Minimization and treatment of this flowback is an important goal of research.

Pumps, currently attaining at the surface level the pressure of about 25 MPa, push the fracking fluid through the perforations into the shale stratum. To begin with, the shale is intersected by a system of natural fractures or rock joints, nearly vertical, which are either tightly closed or filled by calcite or other minerals. They are typically 15–50 cm apart. The shale is also intersected by numerous finer faults and inclined slip planes. The shale contains weak near horizontal bedding planes with sub-millimeter spacing, which have higher permeability and higher concentration of kerogen filled Nano-voids. The first, large, hydraulically produced cracks must be roughly normal to the horizontal wellbore, since it is always drilled in the direction of the minimum tectonic stress. No horizontal cracks are expected to form since the overburden pressure exceeds the tectonic stresses.

Most of the gas in gas shale, mainly methane, is contained in kerogen-filled nanopores of diameters from 0.5 nm to about 10 nm. Drilled cores brought to the surface reveal the total gas content of shale, and thus it is estimated that at most 15 %, and often as little as 5 %, of the gas content of the shale stratum gets extracted (percentages as high as 50% have been rumored but probably are rare local aberrations).
(1)

([1])Congrui Jin • Gianluca Cusatis: New Frontiers in Oil and Gas Exploration. Springer International Publishing Switzerland 2016. P 436: 438

7. Drilling Techniques

If we consider a well trajectory from surface to total depth (TD), it is helpful to look at the shallow section and the intermediate and reservoir intervals separately.

The shallow section, usually referred to as top hole, consists of rather unconsolidated sediments, hence the formation strength is low and drilling parameters and equipment have to be selected accordingly.

The reservoir section is more consolidated and is the main objective to which the well is being drilled, hence the drilling process has to ensure that any productive interval is not damaged. [1]

7.1. Top hole drilling

For the very first section of the borehole, a base from which to commence drilling is required. In a land location, this will be a cemented 'cellar' in which a conductor or

---

[1]Frank Jahn, Mark Cook and Mark Graham: HYDROCARBON EXPLORATION AND PRODUCTION. 2ND EDITION. Elsevier B.V. 2008. P 62

stove pipe will be piled prior to the rig moving in. The cellar will later accommodate the 'Christmas tree' (an arrangement of seals and valves to control production), once the well has been completed and the rig has moved off location.

As in the construction industry, piling of the conductor is done by dropping weights onto the pipe or using a hydraulic hammer until no further penetration occurs. In an offshore environment, the conductor is either piled (e.g. on a platform) or a large-diameter hole is actually drilled, into which the conductor is lowered and cemented. Once the drill bit has drilled below the conductor the well is said to have been spudded.

The top hole will usually be drilled with a large-diameter bit (between 22 and 27 in. diameter). The drill bit (roller cone type) will be designed to drill predominantly soft formations. As a result of the hole diameter and the rapid penetration rate, vast quantities of drilled formation will have to be treated and removed from the mud circulation system. Often the ROP will be reduced to allow adequate removal of cuttings and conditioning of mud. In some cases, the problem is alleviated by first drilling a pilot hole with a smaller diameter bit (12.25 in.) and later redrilling the section to the required size using a hole opener. This is essentially a larger diameter drill bit above the smaller diameter bit. Hole openers are also run if the hole has to be logged (most logging tools are not designed for diameters above 17.5 in.) and if accurate directional drilling is required.

A surface casing is finally cemented to prevent hole collapse and protect shallow aquifers. [1]

---

[1] Frank Jahn, Mark Cook and Mark Graham: HYDROCARBON EXPLORATION AND PRODUCTION. 2ND EDITION. Elsevier B.V. 2008. P 63

7.2. Intermediate and reservoir section

Between the top hole and the reservoir section, in most cases, an intermediate section will need to be drilled. This section consists of more consolidated rocks than the top hole. The deviation angle is often increased significantly in this interval to reach the subsurface target, and lateral departures from the surface co-ordinates may reach several kilometers. Based on pore pressure prediction (from seismic or measured data from offset wells) the mud weight has to be determined. The pressure exerted by the mud column has to exceed the formation pressure in order to maintain overbalance and prevent the hole from collapsing but has to be lower than the fracture pressure of the formation. If the formation strength is exceeded, fracturing may occur, resulting in mud losses and formation damage.

Borehole/formation stability is the realm of geomechanics. Challenges in well planning arise when rock strength and thus borehole stability show considerable variations depending on hole angle and direction, as shown in the Figure. In this example, the small difference between fracture gradient and collapse gradient at high deviation may require a revision of the initially planned well trajectory through the intermediate and/or reservoir section.

An intermediate casing is usually set above the reservoir in order to protect the water-bearing, hydrostatically pressured zones from influx of possibly over pressured

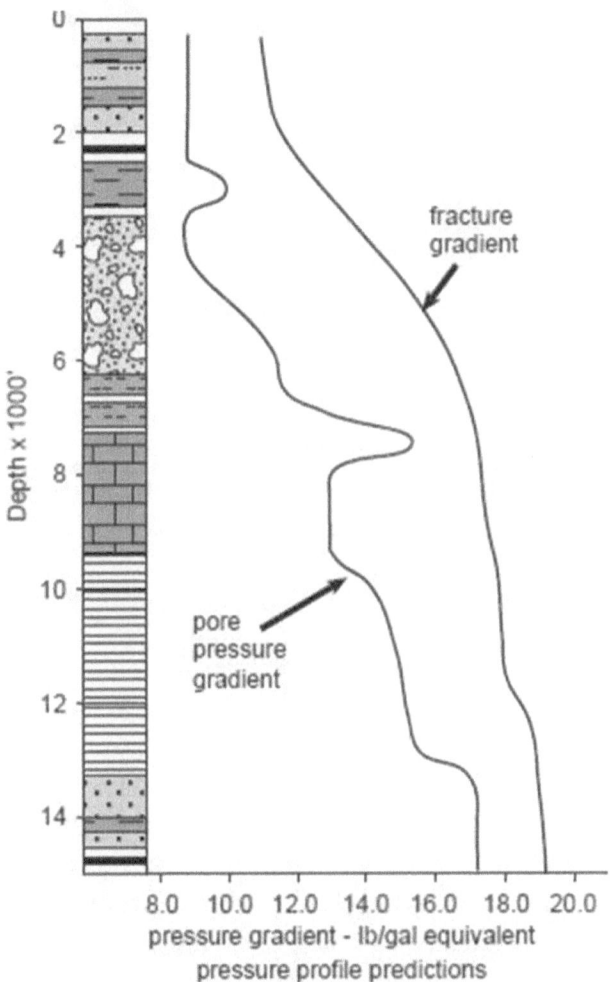

pressure profile predictions

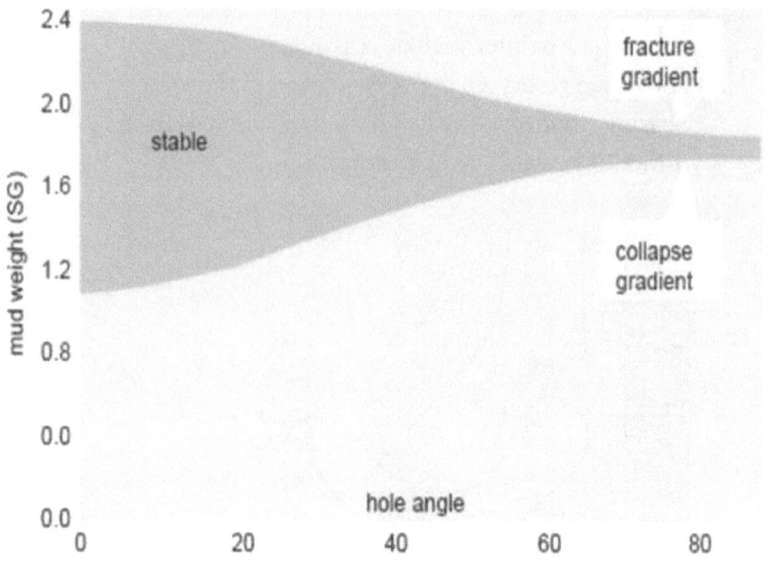

hydrocarbons and to guarantee the integrity of the wellbore above the objective zone. In mature fields where production has been ongoing for many years, the reservoir may show depletion pressures considerably lower than the hydrostatically pressured zones above.

Before continuing to examine the aspects of drilling through the reservoir, remember that the reservoir is the prime objective of the well and a very significant future asset to the company. If the drilling process has impaired the formation, production may be deferred or totally lost. In exploration wells, the information from logging and testing may not be sufficient to fully evaluate the prospect if the hole is not on gauge, necessitating sidetracking or even an additional well.

On the other hand, there is considerable scope to improve productivity and information value of the well by carefully selecting the appropriate technology and practices.

In some areas such as the Central North Sea, offshore Canada, and onshore California, high pressure high temperature (HPHT) accumulations are present. Wells may encounter reservoir temperatures in excess of 370F (190C) and pressures above 15,000 psi. These are challenging conditions for drilling fluids, mud motors, gauges and logging tools. In particular, components such as batteries, sensors, electronics and seal elastomers had to be specifically developed for these extreme conditions. [1]

7.3. Directional drilling

Directional drilling is usually done with a rotary steerable system. A downhole steering and control unit is located in the near-bit assembly. A set of small electronically controlled rotating stabilizer pads (actuators)

---

[1] Frank Jahn, Mark Cook and Mark Graham: HYDROCARBON EXPLORATION AND PRODUCTION. 2ND EDITION. Elsevier B.V. 2008. P 63: 65

exert a continuous directional force onto a drive shaft which orients the drill bit into the desired

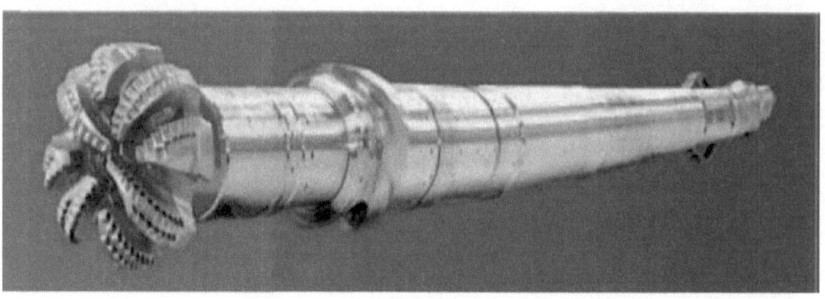

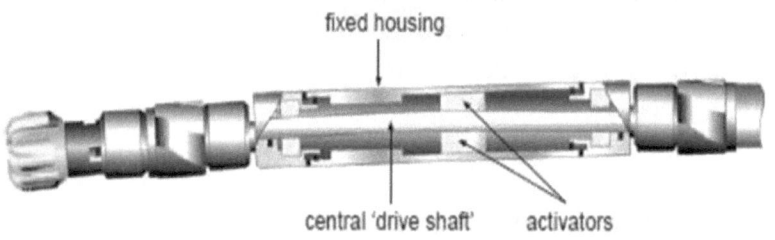

Gyro/Data *Inc.*

direction. The drill string is rotated at the same time, allowing hole cleaning.

A control unit near the bit ensures that the hole angle is not increased or decreased rapidly creating 'dog legs' which will result in excessive torque and drag. The rotary steerable system is combined with logging tools in the drill string close to the bit, allowing a continuous optimization of the well trajectory.

Mud turbines and mud motors are also used for directional drilling. Rotational movement of the drill string is restricted to the motor or turbine section, whilst the rest of the drill string moves by 'sliding' or being rotated at a lower speed to ensure hole cleaning. In the example of the turbine shown in the Figure, the mud is pumped between the rotor and the stator section, inducing a rotational movement which is transmitted onto the drill bit. Motors and turbines are being replaced by the rotary steerable system for cost and operational reasons. Their use is increasingly limited to such applications as kicking off a sidetrack or where a sharp change in angle is required in a short-radius horizontal well.

Advances in drilling and completion technology today allow us to construct complicated wells along 3D trajectories. In addition to vertical wells, directional drilling allows us to build, maintain or drop hole angle and to turn the drill bit into different directions. Thus, we are able to optimize the well path in terms of reservoir quality, production or injection requirements. Sometimes constraints at the surface (e.g. built-up areas) or subsurface (e.g. shallow gas, faults, lenticular reservoirs) may require a particular well trajectory to be followed.

The steering of the well is supported by the stabilizers which form part of the drill string. The blades can be activated and deactivated from the surface depending on whether the angle is to be maintained, increased or decreased.

High deviation angles (above 60) may cause excessive drag or torque whilst drilling and will also make it difficult to later service the well with standard wireline tools.

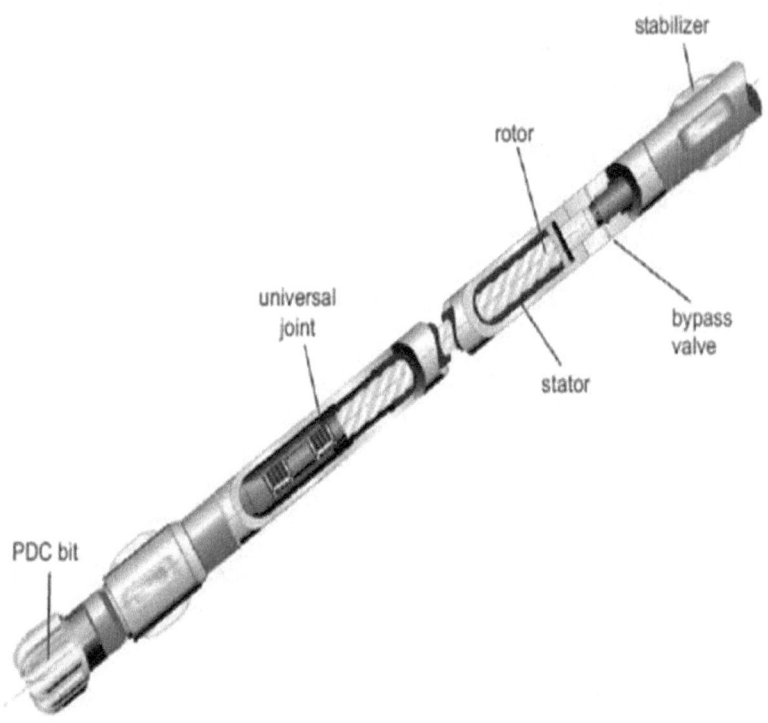

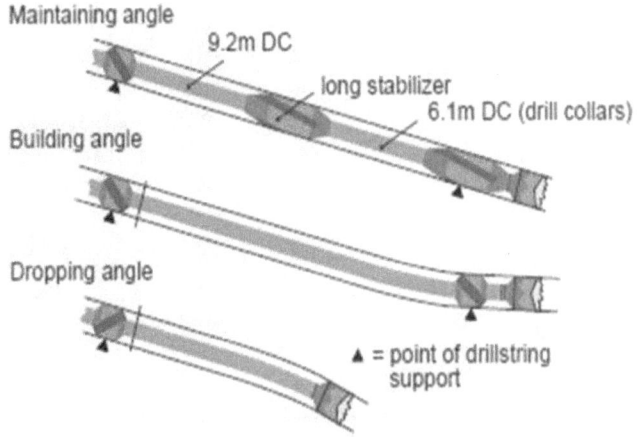

Types of assemblies for directional drilling.

7.4. Horizontal drilling

Given the lateral distribution of reservoir rock or reservoir fluids, a horizontal well may provide the optimum trajectory. the Figure shows the types of horizontal wells being drilled. The build-up rate of angle is the main distinction from a drilling point of view. Medium radius wells are preferred since they can be drilled, logged and completed with fairly standard equipment. The horizontal drilling target can be controlled within a vertical window of less than 2 m.

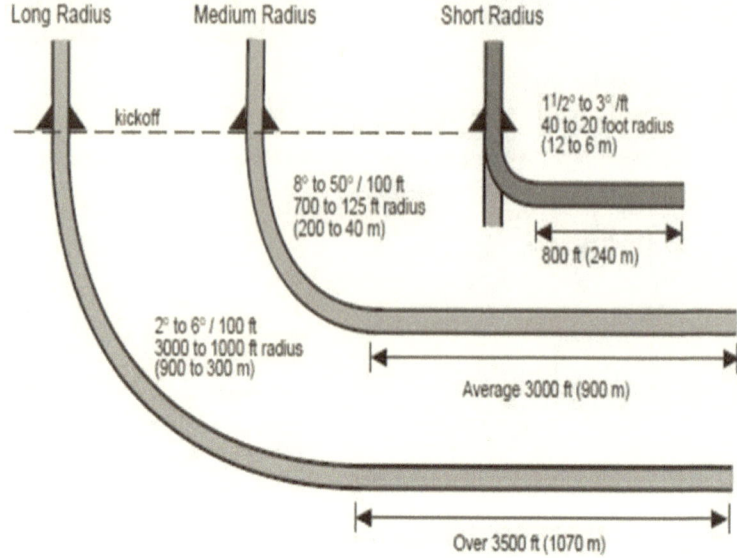

The success of horizontal wells was largely dependent on the development of tools which relay the subsurface position of the drill bit in real time to the drill floor.

Improvements in this technology have greatly improved the accuracy with which well trajectories can be targeted. MWD is achieved by the insertion of a sonde into the drill string close to the bit. Initially providing only directional data, the tools have been improved to the point where petrophysical data gathering (gamma ray [GR], resistivity, density and porosity) can be carried out whilst drilling.

Most reservoirs are characterized by marked lateral changes in reservoir quality corresponding to variations in lithology.

Computing tools now commercially available allow the modelling of expected formation responses 'ahead of the bit'.

This is possible in areas where a data set of the formations to be drilled has been acquired in previous wells. The expected GR and density response is then simulated and compared to the corresponding signature picked up by the tool. Thus, in theory, it is possible to direct the bit towards the high-quality parts of the reservoir.

Resistivity measurements enable the driller to steer the bit above a hydrocarbon water contact (HCWC), a technique used, for example, to produce thin oil rims.

These techniques, known as geosteering, are increasingly being applied to field development optimization. Geosteering also relies on the availability of high-quality seismic and possibly detailed paleontological sampling. [1]

---

[1] Frank Jahn, Mark Cook and Mark Graham: HYDROCARBON EXPLORATION AND PRODUCTION. 2ND EDITION. Elsevier B.V. 2008. P 65: 67

7.5. Multilateral wells

Drilling a number of holes, branching from a central borehole, is an attractive option in the following cases:

- where reservoir productivity is low but can be significantly improved by

increasing the reservoir surface area exposed to the well

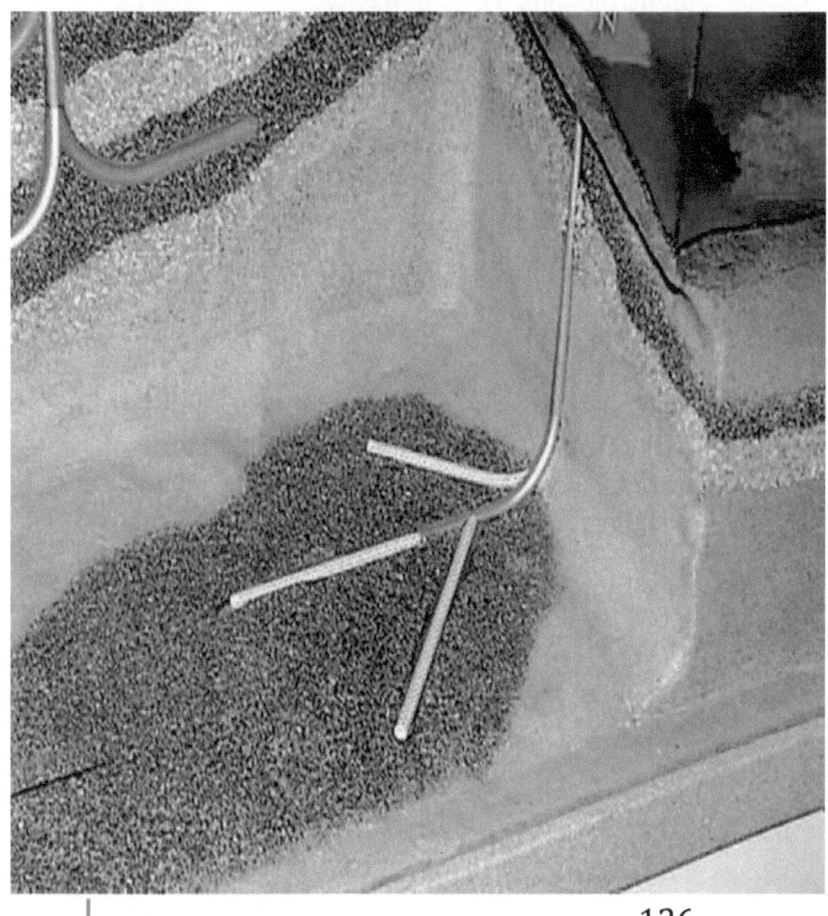

_ in reservoirs which are lenticular

_ where reservoir layers are vertically segregated by permeability barriers.

Whilst drilling and, in particular, completing is more complex, multilateral wells have the advantage that they only require one borehole from the surface. If there are no spare conductors on the platform, this is an attractive option.

In mature fields, multilaterals are often best suited to drain remaining pockets of hydrocarbons. In subsea developments, multilaterals can offer a substantial cost advantage over conventional wells.

To commence drilling of each branch, either a rotary steerable system or a whipstock are used. The latter is a curved steel wedge which is inserted into the borehole, forcing the drilling assembly in the planned azimuth. [1]

7.6. Horizontal Wells

Horizontal wells were drilled as far back as the 1950s but gained great popularity from the 1980s onwards as directional drilling technology progressed and cost pressure

---

[1]Frank Jahn, Mark Cook and Mark Graham: HYDROCARBON EXPLORATION AND PRODUCTION. 2ND EDITION. Elsevier B.V. 2008. P 68: 69

mounted. Horizontal wells have potential advantages over vertical or deviated wells for three main reasons

_ increased exposure to the reservoir giving higher productivity indices (PIs)

_ ability to connect laterally discontinuous features, for example fractures, fault blocks

_ changing the geometry of drainage, for example being parallel to fluid contacts.

The increased exposure to the reservoir results from the long horizontal sections which can be attained (sections many kilometers in length are now routine in many fields). Because the PI is a function of the length of reservoir drained by a well, horizontal wells can give higher productivities in laterally extensive reservoirs. As an estimate of the initial potential benefit of horizontal wells, one can use a rough rule of thumb, the productivity improvement factor (PIF) which compares the initial productivity of a horizontal well to that of a vertical well in the same reservoir, during early time radial flow:

$$PIF = \frac{L}{h}\sqrt{\frac{k_v}{k_h}}$$

where L is the length of the reservoir; h the height of the reservoir; k_h the horizontal permeability of the reservoir; k_v the vertical permeability of the reservoir. The geometry and reservoir quality have a very important influence on whether horizontal wells will realize a benefit compared to a vertical well, as demonstrated by the following example.

In the case of the very low vertical permeability, the horizontal well actually produces at a lower rate than the vertical well. Each of these examples assumes that the reservoir is a block, with uniform properties. The ultimate recovery from the horizontal well in the above examples is unlikely to be different to that of the vertical well, and the major benefit is in the accelerated production achieved by the horizontal well.

The PIF estimate is only a qualitative check on the potential initial benefit of a horizontal well. The stabilized flowrate benefits of horizontal wells compared to vertical wells are more rigorously handled by relationships derived by Joshi (ref. Horizontal Well Technology, Pennwell, 1991). Also, in high permeability reservoirs there is actually a diminishing return of production rate on the length of well drilled, due to increasing friction pressure drops with increasing well length, shown schematically in the Figure.

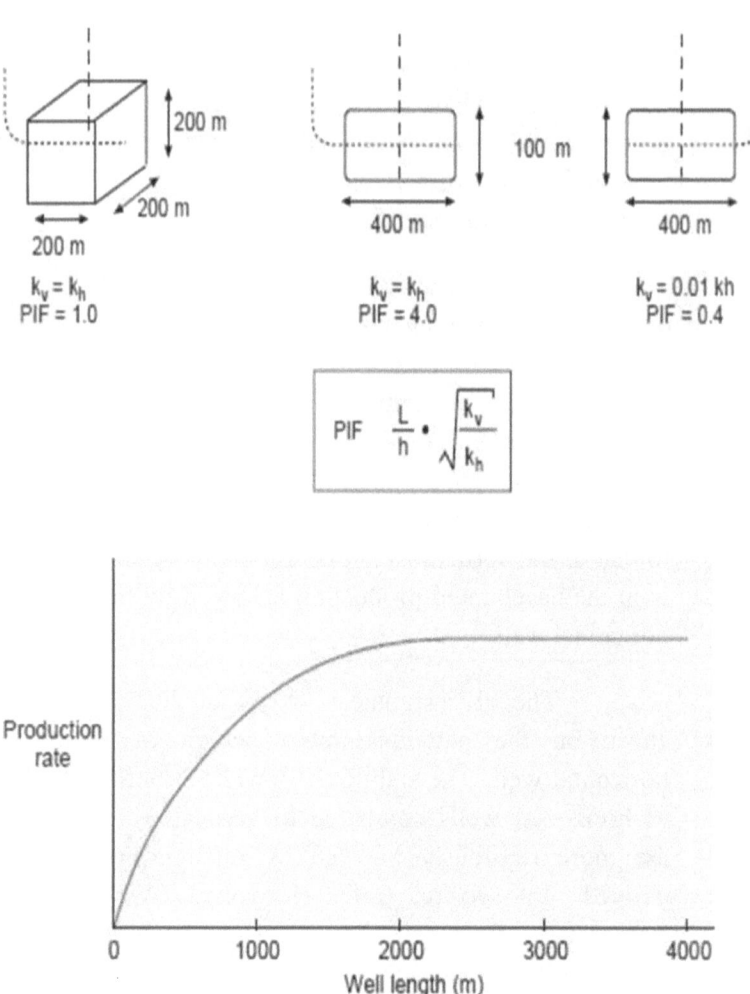

The exact relationship will depend on both fluid and reservoir properties and will be investigated during well planning. Poor completion practices may exacerbate the problem as the lower drawdown on the toe of the well compared to the heel may prevent proper clean-up of mud, filter cake and completion fluids.

Horizontal wells have a large potential to connect laterally discontinuous features in heterogeneous or discontinuous reservoirs. If the reservoir quality is locally poor, the subsequent section of the reservoir may be of better quality, providing a healthy productivity for the well. If the reservoir is faulted or fractured a horizontal well may connect a series of fault blocks or natural fractures in a manner which would require many vertical wells. The ultimate recovery of a horizontal well is likely to be significantly greater than for a single vertical well.

The third main application of horizontal wells is to reduce the effects of coning and cusping by changing the geometry of drainage close to the well. For example, a horizontal producing well may be placed along the crest of a tilted fault block to remain as far away from the advancing oil–water contact as possible during water drive. An additional advantage is that if the PI for the horizontal well is larger, then the same oil production can be achieved at much lower drawdown, therefore minimizing the effect of coning or cusping. The result is that oil production is achieved with significantly less water production, which reduces processing costs and assists in maintaining reservoir pressure. Horizontal wells have a particularly strong advantage in thin oil columns (say, less than 40m thick), which would be prone to coning if developed using conventional wells. The unwanted fluid in oil rim development may be water or gas,

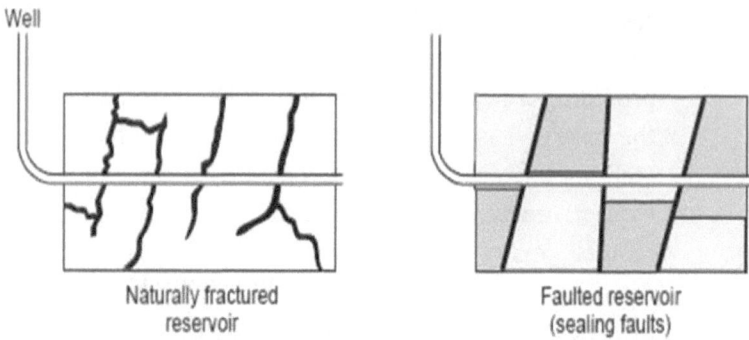

Naturally fractured reservoir

Faulted reservoir (sealing faults)

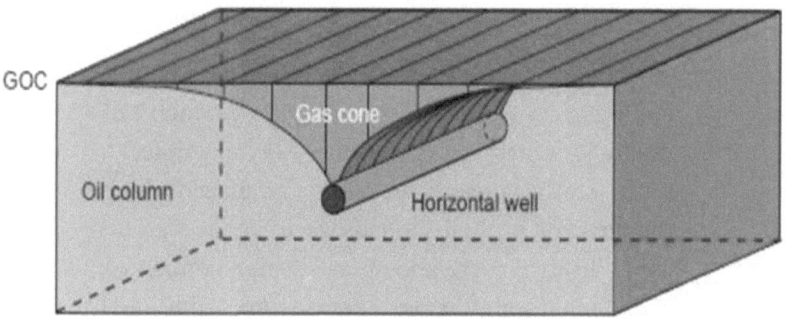

or both. The distortion of the fluid interface near the horizontal well is referred to as cresting rather than coning, due to the shape of the interface. The Figure shows a schematic view of gas cresting from an overlying gas cap in an oil reservoir. [1]

Advances in drilling and completion technologies have placed horizontal wells among the techniques used to improve production performance. For example, in the case of gas cap or bottom water drive, horizontal wells prevent coning without introducing the flow restriction seen in partial penetration wells. Horizontal drilling is also efficient to increase the well surface area for fluid withdrawal, thus improving the productivity. [2]

7.7. Extended reach drilling

An extended reach well is loosely defined as having a horizontal displacement of at least twice the vertical depth. With current technology, a ratio of over 4 (horizontal displacement/vertical depth) can be achieved.

Extended reach drilling (ERD) wells are technically more difficult to drill and because of the degree of engineering required for each well, the term 'designer well' is frequently used.

---

[1] Frank Jahn, Mark Cook and Mark Graham: HYDROCARBON EXPLORATION AND PRODUCTION. 2ND EDITION. Elsevier B.V. 2008. P 234: 237

[2] JOHN CUBITT: Handbook of Petroleum Exploration and Production. E l s e v i e r Science B.V. 2002. P 81

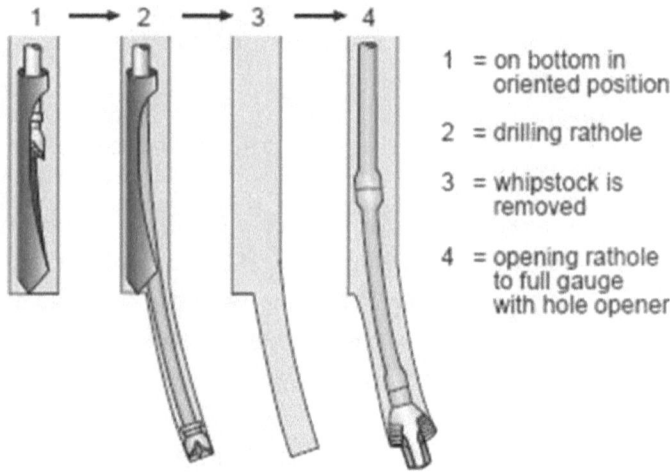

1 = on bottom in oriented position
2 = drilling rathole
3 = whipstock is removed
4 = opening rathole to full gauge with hole opener

Kicking off with a whipstock.

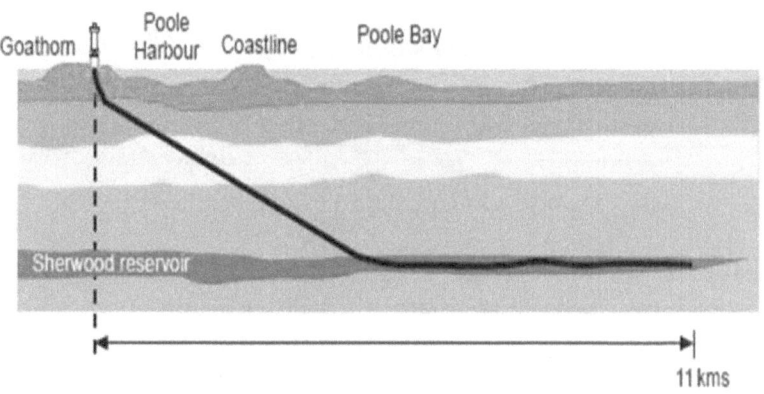

ERD will be considered:

_ where surface restrictions exist

_ where marginal accumulations are located several miles from existing platforms/ clusters

_ where ERD allows a reduction in the number of platforms required.

The high deviation (often up to 85) and the long horizontal displacement expose the drill string to extreme drag and torque. Hole cleaning (cutting removal) and cementing of casing is more difficult due to the increased effect of gravity forces compared to low-angle wells. Thus, ERD wells usually require heavier and better equipped rigs compared to standard wells and take longer to drill. Top drive systems are routinely employed in combination with rotary steerable systems.

Not surprisingly, costs are several times higher than conventional wells. Nevertheless, overall project economics may favor ERD over other development options. For example, BP developed the offshore part of the Wytch Farm Oilfield (which is located under Poole Harbor in Dorset, UK) from an onshore location.

The wells targeted the reservoir at a vertical depth of 1500m with a lateral displacement of over 11,000m. The alternative was to build a drilling location on an artificial island in Poole Bay. ERD probably saved a considerable amount of money and advanced first oil by several years. Offshore, subsea satellite development may be a viable alternative to ERD wells. [1]

7.8. Slim hole drilling

Slim hole drilling has been used by the mining industry for a number of years.

Recently, the oil industry has been developing rigs, drill string components and logging tools that will allow smaller diameter holes and completions. One definition used for 'slim holes' is 'a well in which 90% or more of the length has a diameter of 7 in. or less'. In principle, slim hole drilling has the potential to drill wells at greatly reduced cost (estimates range from 40 to 60%). The cost reductions accrue from several sources:

_ less site preparation

_ easier equipment mobilization

_ reduction in the number of consumables (drill bits, cement, muds, fuel)

_ less cuttings to dispose of

_ smaller equipment.

A slim hole rig weighs about one-fifth of a conventional rig and its small size can open

---

[1]Frank Jahn, Mark Cook and Mark Graham: HYDROCARBON EXPLORATION AND PRODUCTION. 2ND EDITION. Elsevier B.V. 2008. P 69: 71

new frontiers by making exploration economic in environmentally sensitive or inaccessible areas.

The following table highlights the potential of slim hole wells:

Type of Rig	Conventional	Slim Hole
Hole diameter (in.)	8.5	3–6
Drill string weight (tons)	40	5–7
Rig weight (tons)	80	10
Drill site area (%)	100	25
Installed power (kW)	350	70–100
Mud tank capacity (bbl)	500	30
Hole volume (bbl/1000 ft)	60	6–12
Crew size	25–30	12–15

The greatly reduced hole volume of slim hole wells can lead to problems if an influx is experienced. The maximum depth drillable with slim hole configurations is another current limitation of this technology.

Some slim hole rigs were adapted from units employed by mining exploration companies and are designed to allow continuous coring rather than breaking the formation into cuttings. These rigs are sometimes employed for data gathering wells in exploration ventures. They are ideally suited for remote locations since they can be transported in segments by helicopter. [1]

---

[1] Frank Jahn, Mark Cook and Mark Graham: HYDROCARBON EXPLORATION AND PRODUCTION. 2ND EDITION. Elsevier B.V. 2008. P 71: 72

8. Well Planning and costs
8.2. Well planning

The drilling of a well involves a major investment, ranging from a few million US$ for an onshore well to 100 million US$ plus for a Deepwater exploration well.

Well engineering is aimed at maximizing the value of this investment by employing the most appropriate technology and business processes, to drill a 'fit for purpose' well, at the minimum cost, without compromising safety or environmental standards. Successful drilling engineering requires the integration of many disciplines and skills.

Successful drilling projects will require extensive planning. Usually, wells are drilled with one, or a combination, of the following objectives:

_ to gather information

_ to produce hydrocarbons

_ to inject gas or water to maintain reservoir pressure or sweep out oil

_ to dispose of water, drill cuttings or CO2 (sequestration).

139

To optimize the design of a well it is desirable to have as accurate a picture as possible of the subsurface. Therefore, a number of disciplines will have to provide information prior to the design of the well trajectory and before a drilling rig and specific equipment can be selected.

The subsurface team will define optimum locations for the planned wells to penetrate the reservoir and in consultation with the well engineer agree on the desired trajectory through the objective sequence. In discussions with production and well engineers maximum hole inclination and required wellbore diameter will be determined. Wellhead locations, well design and trajectory are aimed at minimizing the combined costs of well construction and seabed/surface facilities, whilst maximizing production.

The accuracy of the parameters used in the well planning process will depend on the knowledge of the field or the region. Particularly during exploration drilling and the early stages of field development considerable uncertainty in subsurface data will prevail. It is important that the uncertainties are clearly spelled out and preferably quantified. Potential risks and problems expected or already encountered in offset wells (earlier wells drilled in the area) should be incorporated into the design of the planned well. This is often achieved by using a decision tree approach in the well planning phase. The optimum well design balances risk, uncertainty and cost with overall project value.

The basis for the well design is captured in a comprehensive document. This is then 'translated' into a drilling program.

In summary, the well engineer will be able to design and cost the well in detail using the information obtained from the petroleum engineers, geoscientists and production engineers. In particular, he will plan the setting depth and ratings for the various casing strings, cementing program, mud weights and mud types required during drilling, and select an appropriate rig and related hardware, for example drill bits. [1]

8.2. Costs of Drilling

An increase in depth increases drilling costs. Costs increase exponentially with depth, even for a "normal," trouble-free well. An increase in depth can also increase the chances of mechanical problems, which adds to the cost of drilling.

---

[1]Frank Jahn, Mark Cook and Mark Graham: HYDROCARBON EXPLORATION AND PRODUCTION. 2ND EDITION. Elsevier B.V. 2008. P 47: 48

Increased depth also reduces available information about potential reservoirs about quality of crude oil and quantity available (proven reserves). Risks increase with uncertainties about reservoir quantity and quality available.

Costs of drilling depend on the kind of oil and what potential energy the oil possesses by virtue of its initial pressure in its reservoir, and by the amount of dissolved gas it may contain. In many cases the crude may have enough potential energy to permit a well to flow large quantities of oil to the surface without any artificial assistance, such as use of gas or water injection. (This is quite prevalent in oil wells in the Middle East.) But when oil

cannot flow unaided, or when the pressure in the reservoir has decreased to a pressure that is too low to be economical, costly mechanisms that lift oil to the ground surface must be employed. Low pressure in the reservoir and low gas content generally go together. This kind of crude, therefore, must be handled in a different manner.

The daily rates of offshore drilling rigs vary by their capability and market availability. With deep-water, drilling rig rates of around $420,000/day were reported in 2010. A high-pressure, high-temperature well of duration 100 days can cost about $30 million.

Onshore wells can be considerably cheaper, particularly if the field is at a shallow depth, where costs range from less than $1 million to $15 million for deep and difficult wells.

Statistical information for the period 2002 to 2007 on the costs of crude oil and natural gas well drills are reported by U.S. Energy Information as follows: [1]

---

[1] Hussein K. Abdel-Aal, Mohammed A. Alsahlawi: Petroleum Economics and Engineering. Third Edition. Taylor & Francis Group, LLC. 2014. P 231:232

	GraphClear	2002	2003	2004	2005	2006	2007	View History
Thousand Dollars per Well								
All (real*)	☐	1,011.9	1,127.4	1,528.5	1,522.3	1,801.3	3,481.8	1960–2007
All (nominal)	☐	1,054.2	1,199.5	1,673.1	1,720.7	2,101.7	4,171.7	1960–2007
Crude oil (nominal)	☐	882.8	1,037.3	1,441.8	1,920.4	2,238.6	4,000.4	1960–2007
Natural gas (nominal)	☐	991.9	1,106.0	1,716.4	1,497.6	1,936.2	3,906.9	1960–2007
Dry holes (nominal)	☐	1,673.4	2,065.1	1,977.3	2,392.9	2,664.6	6,131.2	1960–2007
Dollars per Foot								
All (real*)	☐	187.46	203.25	267.28	271.16	324.00	574.46	1960–2007
All (nominal)	☐	195.31	216.27	292.57	306.50	378.03	688.30	1960–2007
Crude oil (nominal)	☐	194.55	221.13	298.45	314.36	402.45	717.13	1960–2007
Natural gas (nominal)	☐	175.78	189.95	284.78	280.03	348.36	604.06	1960–2007
Dry holes (nominal)	☐	284.17	345.94	327.91	429.92	479.33	1,132.09	1960–2007

Source: U.S. EIA: Annual Energy Outlook 2013, Release Dates: April 15, May 2, 2013.

8.3. Operating Costs

Net profits associated with operating a rig are determined from the contract day rate less the daily operating costs. Generally speaking, deep water, high-spec, international rigs cost more to operate than shallow water, low-spec, domestic rigs. Rig size and age, port infrastructure, scale economies related to a contractor's regional presence, market competition, and the availability of goods and services are primary factors that impact operating cost.

8.4. Operating Margin

Operating margin is the ratio of operating income (earnings before interest and taxes) to revenue and is an aggregate measure of the cost structure of the firm. Firms with higher operating margins have larger net earnings per dollar of revenue than firms with lower margins. Firms with older fleets or a large number of stacked rigs are expected to have lower operating margins than firms with younger or more active rigs. A statistically significant negative relationship exists between the percentage of the fleet that was stacked in 4Q2011 and operating margin, but many other factors are responsible for operating margin and the relationship only explains a small proportion of the variation. [1]

8.5. Business Segments

Several companies operate offshore rigs as a small, non-core part of their business operations. Saipem, Maersk Drilling, Nabors,

---

[1] Mark J.Kaiser, Brian F.Snyder: The Offshore Drilling Industry and Rig Construction in the Gulf of Mexico, Springer-Verlag London 2013. P 134: 135

Petrobras, and Oil and Natural Gas Corporation (ONGC) of India generate less than half of their revenues from offshore drilling. Saipem derives the majority of its revenue from offshore construction, Maersk Drilling is a subsidiary of the shipping conglomerate A.P. Moeller Maersk, Nabors is primarily an onshore drilling contractor, and Petrobras and ONGC are National Oil Companies. Other firms such as Aban, Fred Olsen Energy, COSL, and Hercules also have investments in other industries, but these investments do not generate more than 25 % of the firm's revenue. Aban has investments in wind energy, Fred Olsen Energy in offshore construction, COSL is an integrated offshore oilfield services company, and Hercules operates a lift boat division. [1]

In 2012, Singapore dominated jackup construction, Korea was building most of the world's drillships, and semisubmersible newbuilds were split between China, Mexico and Singapore. From 2005 to 2012, Keppel and Sembcorp were dominant in jackup and semi construction, while Samsung and Daewoo were dominant in drillship construction. Competitive advantages change over time and geographic redistribution will arise, but for the near-term

---

[1] Mark J.Kaiser, Brian F.Snyder: The Offshore Drilling Industry and Rig Construction in the Gulf of Mexico, Springer-Verlag London 2013. P 137

future these players are expected to maintain a dominant position in the industry. [1]

---

[1] Mark J.Kaiser, Brian F.Snyder: The Offshore Drilling Industry and Rig Construction in the Gulf of Mexico, Springer-Verlag London 2013. P 154

9. Contracts

The actual well costs are divided into

_ Fixed costs: casing and tubulars, logging, cementing, drill bits, mobilization charges, rig move

_ Daily costs: contractor services, rig time, consumables

_ Overheads: offices, salaries, pensions, health care, travel.

A fairly significant charge is usually made by the drilling contractor to modify and prepare the rig for a specific drilling campaign. This is known as a mobilization cost. A similar charge will cover 'once off' expenses related to terminating the operations for a particular client and is called a demobilization cost. These costs can be significant, say 5–10 million US$. he actual costs of a well show considerable variations and are dependent on a number of factors, for example

_ type of well (exploration, appraisal, development)

_ well trajectory (vertical, deviated, horizontal, multilateral)

_ total depth

_ subsurface environment (temperatures, pressures, corrosiveness of fluids)

_ type and rating of rig

_ type of operation (land, marine)

_ infrastructure available, transport and logistics

_ climate and geography (tropical, arctic, remoteness of location).

Most companies hire a drilling contractor to supply equipment and manpower rather than having their own rigs and crews. The reasons for this are threefold:

_ a considerable investment is required to build/buy a rig

_ rig and crew need to be maintained and paid regardless of the operational requirements and activities of the company

_ drilling contractors can usually operate more cheaply and efficiently than a company which carries out drilling operations as a non-core activity. Before a contract is awarded a tender procedure is usually carried out. Thus, a number of suitable companies are invited to bid for a specified amount of work. Bids will be evaluated based on price, rig specifications and the past performance of the contractor, with particular attention to their safety record. Several types of contract are used.

9.1. Turnkey contract

This type of contract requires the operator to pay a fixed amount to the contractor upon completion of the well, whilst the contractor furnishes all the material and labor and handles the drilling operations independently. The difficulty with this approach is to ensure that a 'quality well' is delivered to the company since the drilling contractor will want to drill as quickly and cheaply as possible. The contractor therefore should guarantee an agreed measurable quality standard for each well. The guarantee should specify remedial actions which will be implemented should a substandard well be delivered.

9.2. Footage contract

The contractor is paid per foot drilled. Whilst this will provide an incentive to 'make hole' quickly, the same risks are involved as in the turnkey contract. Footage contracts are often used for the section above the prospective reservoir where hole conditions are less crucial from an evaluation or production point of view.

9.3. Incentive contract

This method of running drilling operations has been very successfully applied in recent years and has resulted in considerable cost savings. Various systems are in operation, usually providing a bonus for better than average performance. The contractor agrees with the company on the specifications for the well. Then the 'historic' cost of similar wells which have been drilled in the past is established. This allows estimation of the costs expected for the new well. The contractor will be entirely in charge of drilling the well, and cost savings achieved will be split between company and contractor.

9.4. Day rate contract

As the name implies the company basically rents the rig and crew on a per day basis.

Usually the oil company also manages the drilling operation and has full control over the drilling process. This type of contract actually encourages the contractor to spend as much time as acceptable 'on location'. With increased cost consciousness, day rate contracts have become less favored by most oil companies.

Actual contracts often involve a combination of the above. For instance, an operator may agree to pay footage rates to a certain depth, day rates below that depth, and standby rates for days when the rig is on site, but not drilling.

9.5. Partnering and alliances

In recent years, a new approach to contracting has evolved and is gaining rapid acceptance in the industry. The concept has become known as partnering and can be seen as a progression of the incentive contract. Whilst the previously described contractual arrangements are restricted to a single well project or a small number of wells in which a contractor is paid by a client for the work performed, partnering describes the initiation of a long-term relationship between the asset holder (e.g. an oil company) and the service companies (e.g. drilling contractor and equipment suppliers). It includes the definition and merging of joint business objectives, the sharing of financial risks and rewards and is aimed at an improvement in efficiency and reduction of operating costs. Therefore, a partnering contract will not only address technical issues but also include business process quality management. The latter has proven to result in more efficient and economic use of resources, for instance the setting up of 'joint implementation teams' has replaced the practice of having separate teams in contractor and operator offices, essentially performing the same tasks.

The industry is increasingly acknowledging the value of contractors and service companies in improving their individual core capabilities through alliances, that is a joint venture for a particular project or a number of projects. A lead contractor, for example a drilling company, may form alliances with a number of subcontractors to be able to cover a wider spectrum of activities, for example

completions, workovers and well interventions.
[1]

---

[1]Frank Jahn, Mark Cook and Mark Graham: HYDROCARBON EXPLORATION AND PRODUCTION. 2ND EDITION. Elsevier B.V. 2008. P 79: 81

10. Drilling Rig

Rigs are classified according to type (bottom supported, floating), environmental capacity (harsh, moderate), water depth, and specification (standard, premium). MODUs are classified as bottom-supported or floating rigs. In bottom supported units, the rig is in contact with the seafloor during drilling, while a floating rig floats over the site while it drills, held in position by anchors or equipped with thrusters using dynamic positioning. Bottom supported units are used for shallow-water drilling and include barges, submersibles and jackups Floaters are used for deep water drilling and include semisubmersibles and drillships Jackups, drillships and semisubmersibles comprise the majority of the offshore fleet. [1]

Rigs are classified as harsh or moderate environment units. Harsh environments are characterized by frequent and severe storms as occur during winter in the Northern Hemisphere (North Sea, Norwegian Sea, North Pacific, Eastern Canada). In the Gulf of Mexico and much of Asia, moderate environmental conditions predominate for most of the year, but tropical storms may cause severe weather events. In Brazil, Australia, West Africa and the Persian Gulf, severe weather is rare.

---

[1] Mark J.Kaiser, Brian F.Snyder: The Offshore Drilling Industry and Rig Construction in the Gulf of Mexico, Springer-Verlag London 2013. P 4

In order to work efficiently in a region, a rig must be capable of operating during average 1 year storm conditions and surviving 100 year storm conditions Due to tropical storms, the 100 year storm conditions in the North Sea are similar to conditions in the Gulf of Mexico and Asia; however, 1 year storm conditions are far more severe in the North Sea As a result, harsh and moderate environment rigs differ in maximum operating conditions but do not differ in maximum survival conditions.

Harsh environment units have a number of design modifications to decrease weather related downtime, including increased variable load to reduce the need for resupply, increased airgap to increase wave clearance, and changes in the geometry and spacing of the legs and columns to decrease wind and wave loads. Harsh environment rigs are larger, heavier and more expensive to construct and operate than moderate units. [1]

Drilling operation is mainly of two types, namely, "exploratory" and "development," depending on the purpose and type of wells. Exploratory drilling is usually carried out in the virgin area or in the field

---

[1] Mark J.Kaiser, Brian F.Snyder: The Offshore Drilling Industry and Rig Construction in the Gulf of Mexico, Springer-Verlag London 2013. P 7

whose lithology or subsurface characteristics are unknown.

On the other hand, development drilling is undertaken in a producing field with known reservoir characteristics to enhance production capacity. Based on capacity, depth of drilling, and size of production hole, rigs are categorized as "shallow" or "deep drilling" rig.

Similarly, depending on the type of operation performed, on-land rigs are termed as "drilling" or "workover" rigs. Old wells occasionally require maintenance and recompletion jobs, especially in matured fields that include revival of sick wells, water shutoff jobs, well deepening, sidetracking, fishing, servicing, and so on, that necessitate working over the wells. These jobs are generally done with smaller-sized, cheaper rig with lesser footprint called "workover rig."

A deep drilling rig consists of large-sized modules and high-capacity equipment like draw work, engine, mud pump, mud system, traveling block, crown block, swivel, rotary table, and huge and tall tower called "derrick," apart from varied downhole tubular such as drill pipe, collar, stabilizer, jar, and so on. A shallow or development drilling rig has a smaller-sized module as compared to a deep drilling rig. Workover rigs, on the other hand, are generally truck mounted and have much lesser equipment.

The on-land drilling rigs are of various types, which may be broadly termed as mobile rig, desert rig on wheels, and rig with high floor masts and substructure, all of which are elaborated as follows:

1. Mobile rig: This type of rig is mounted on wheeled carrier and has telescopic mast, which can be driven to the desired location along with equipment, engines, and other accessories. It is used for drilling shallow wells. Rig move time ranges between 16 and 24 h within a distance of 4–5 km.

2. Desert rig on wheels: There are various combinations of rig types depending on capacity, need, varying (heavy) loads on wheels, partially or fully disassembled units, and so forth for which rig move time would also vary. Desert rig on wheels that moves with mast in erect condition takes around 1–2 days for rig move within the same area. Desert rig that moves with mast down condition takes around 3 – 4 days.

3. Rigs with high floor mast and substructure: These are usually higher-capacity rigs used for drilling deeper wells. The rig components are dismantled and transported to the new location by heavy-duty trucks and trailers. Rig move time varies from 1 to 2 weeks depending on the design and capacity of the rig. The current study specifies rig move activities of 1500/2000 HP desert electrical rig on wheels *with fully*

disassembled units (drilling depth capacity—16,000/20,000 ft). [1]

10.1. Platform rig

The decision to use a platform rig should be made prior to the design of the platform. This decision would be influenced by size of field, depth of production, radius of drainage of platform, volume of production, availability of rigs and water depth.

The platform rig would consist of the basic rig components with the living accommodations being part of the platform. This would require additional space and strength to handle the loads imposed. The day cost of this type rig would be less than others but could be offset by the additional expense of the platform. The rig would be, perhaps, a land rig that would be loaded on a barge and towed to the platform. It would then be hoisted on to the platform and positioned over the well template for drilling. [2]

10.2. Jackup rig

The decisions to use a jackup rig would be influenced by the same actors, but generally a lesser number of wells and shallow water would be strongly in favor of the jackup.

---

[1] Sanjib Chowdhury: Optimization and Business Improvement Studies in Upstream Oil and Gas Industry. John Wiley & Sons, Inc. 2016. P 138
[2] Ellis H.Austin: Drilling Engineering, International Human Resources Development Corporation • Boston D. Reidel Publishing Company, 1983. P 198

The platform design should allow sufficient room to position the jackup around the platform without damaging it. This would require the operator to look at a particular rig and sign a contract for this rig in order to assure the compatibility of the two.

The rig would be spotted near the platform with tugs and work boats. The rig anchor system would be put out and the tugs would assist in spotting the rig over the platform.

The rig anchor pattern should insure good holding power and not interfere with the normal operations of the platform such as pipelines, crew and work boats, etc. Anchor piles are sometimes installed on the platform to reduce the anchor-handling problem. [1]

10.3. Semisubmersibles

The increased depth of operational waters has been met with the semisubmersibles. The development of subsea equipment has been such that the continued use of the semis is insured. [2]

---

[1]Ellis H.Austin: Drilling Engineering, International Human Resources Development Corporation • Boston D. Reidel Publishing Company, 1983. P 199
[2]Ellis H.Austin: Drilling Engineering, International Human Resources Development Corporation • Boston D. Reidel Publishing Company, 1983. P 201

The semi (or floater, as it is sometimes referred to) is towed to the location buoy and spotted. The tugs will run the anchor pattern that has been previously selected for minimum interference with operations and weather. The semisubmersible will then be positioned over the proper location and maintain its position automatically within preset limits. 201

Some are self-propelled or have thrusters to assist in towing. The self-propelled speed is generally low, and some government regulations require tugs.

The semisubmersibles have very good motion characteristics that permit drilling operations to continue in waves of 35 to 40 ft high. Wind and current forces tend to push the unit off location. This calls for a heavy mooring system that uses chains (instead of wire rope) and 45,000 lb anchors. This system requires good handling. [1]

In the United States, the Coast Guard has been assigned the responsibility for developing measures to ensure the safety of life at sea. The American Bureau of Shipping (ABS) determines the maximum safe draft to which a drilling unit may be loaded and requires that a visible marking be placed on the vessel at this draft. This maximum draft, or load line, is

---

[1] Ellis H.Austin: Drilling Engineering, International Human Resources Development Corporation • Boston D. Reidel Publishing Company, 1983. P 201

indicated by the Plimsoll Mark. Samuel Plimsoll was a member of the British Parliament and was largely responsible for the passage of the British Merchant Shipping Act of 1876. This act called for the placing of a mark at the maximum safe draft in order that all persons on board the vessel could see that it was not overloaded.

10.4. Drillship

Drillship is a ship with the center part hollowed out for drilling activity. This moonpool area is positioned by the ships power system and maintained within predetermined limits. Drill ships are generally used for the remote wildcat type operations, or in very deep water, or for scientific exploration. The water depth is limited only by its mooring system. 203

Wind, wave, and current action tends to force the unit off its, location. A mooring system of up to 10 anchors and mooring lines could be used to offset forces in any direction. The deployment and recovery of this system is difficult and hazardous. It cannot be accomplished safely in waves of more than 8 to 10 ft. [1]

Drillships are the least expensive floating units to build by conventional mooring. The addition of dynamic positioning increases

---

[1]Ellis H.Austin: Drilling Engineering, International Human Resources Development Corporation • Boston D. Reidel Publishing Company, 1983. P 202: 203

construction cost substantially, but no other alternative is presently available for ultradeep water. The disadvantage to the drills hip is its susceptibility to wave action. **In** 20 to 25 ft waves, the vessel may heave 8 to 10 ft. Drilling operations are usually suspended when heave reaches 5 to 7 ft, so in rough-water areas much of the time is spent waiting on the weather.

10.5. Submersible Rig

The submersible rig is similar to the jackup rig in that they both rest on the bottom. The submersible has hulls on which it floats while being towed to the location. Upon reaching the location, the hulls are flooded and sunk to rest on the bottom. The drilling deck is supported by columns from the hull and is well above the water level. Submersibles have a fixed operating water depth like the jackups and both are limited to drilling in relatively shallow waters. The submersible and jackup rigs provide a very stable platform for operations. [1]

Upon reaching its location, the submersible is submerged by flooding one end of the hull to a reasonable tilt angle. The other end is then flooded, and the vessel is more or less rocked to bottom. The drilling deck must be at such an elevation that the waves can pass safely underneath. On leaving the location, the

---

[1]Ellis H.Austin: Drilling Engineering, International Human Resources Development Corporation • Boston D. Reidel Publishing Company, 1983. P 204

submerging process is reversed. (Some units submerge at a nearly level condition.) Upon reaching the seafloor, the unit is leveled and all tanks are flooded to bring the unit to the desired bearing load on the bottom.

Care must be taken to ballast or deballast the unit evenly about the center line. Too much weight on one side can bring the unit to the surface heeling to one side. Planning can eliminate this problem. A careful operator knows the weight of the unit and how much ballast must be removed to cause it to float freely off bottom. As the unit starts to break suction from the seafloor, observant rig personnel can detect the first movement of the unit as it starts to move with the waves. The deballasting operation should be stopped; the force of the sea gradually causes water to permeate the soil beneath the hull and allows the unit to float. The unit is then raised to the surface. [1]

---

[1] Ellis H.Austin: Drilling Engineering, International Human Resources Development Corporation • Boston D. Reidel Publishing Company, 1983. P 204: 205

11. Offshore Rig Markets

The rig construction industry began in the U.S. in the early 1950s and spread to Europe and Asia in the mid-1970s as offshore exploration increased. At its peak in 1983, 11 U.S. shipyards were engaged in rig construction. Shifts in exploration activity and the general decline in the competitiveness of the U.S. shipbuilding industry led to the entry of new market players, and today, Asia dominates all sectors of the newbuild industry. Since 2000, Asian shipyards have constructed 70 % of all jackups delivered in the world, and almost all semisubmersibles and drillships. The purpose of this chapter is to describe the demand factors and players in rig construction with an emphasis on jackups. We conclude with a brief review of the primary features of construction contracts. [1]

The offshore rig industry is composed of five markets. Cash enters the contract drilling services market when exploration and production (E&P) firms lease rigs from contractors. Contractors use this cash to operate their units, acquire new rigs, and upgrade and maintain their fleet. The newbuild and upgrade markets are the primary mechanisms by which capital leaves the service market.

---

[1] Mark J.Kaiser, Brian F.Snyder: The Offshore Drilling Industry and Rig Construction in the Gulf of Mexico, Springer-Verlag London 2013. P 149

In the contract drilling market, rigs owned and operated by contractors are leased to E&P firms on a day rate basis to drill or service wells. The day rate is the daily price to lease a rig and includes the use of the rig and its crew but does not include most of the other costs associated with drilling and completing a well (e.g., casing, drilling fluids, logistics, well evaluation, etc.). The drilling service industry is the largest and most closely followed of the five markets and drives the activities of investors in the other markets. [1]

The newbuild market uses shipyard labor and capital to convert steel and third-party equipment into rigs. Drilling contractors enter into turnkey contracts with shipyards for the construction and delivery of one or more rigs, or yards may build on speculation. The newbuild market is primarily Asian with major shipyards in Singapore, South Korea, and China.

Rigs operate offshore in a corrosive and hostile environment, and steel and equipment need to be replaced for safe and efficient operations. As a rig ages, its technology also becomes obsolete and upgrades are required to sustain competitiveness and market value. The upgrade market is a ship repair market

---

[1] Mark J.Kaiser, Brian F.Snyder: The Offshore Drilling Industry and Rig Construction in the Gulf of Mexico, Springer-Verlag London 2013. P 29: 30

which both upgrades and maintains rigs. Upgrades improve and modernize rig technology and represent significant capital expenditures.

In the secondhand market, rigs are sold among and between contractors and other market participants. Rigs may be sold for use in the service market, may be converted to another use by the buyer, or sold into the scrap market. Transactions include corporate mergers where all the assets of the firm are purchased, liquidations during bankruptcy where one or more units may be purchased, or conventional sales. [1]

In the scrap market, shipbreaking firms buy rigs on the secondhand market, either directly from contractors or via brokers. Equipment is removed and reused or sold as market conditions and demand permit. Following sale, dismantling occurs and the steel is sold for scrap to steel mills. Rigs in the U.S. may be stored for years until the price of scrap steel is adequate to make dismantling economic, while in international yards, rigs are broken down quickly along with beached ships. The financial value of individual sales in the scrap market is low, and companies do not frequently report income from scrap sales leading to the

---

[1] Mark J.Kaiser, Brian F.Snyder: The Offshore Drilling Industry and Rig Construction in the Gulf of Mexico, Springer-Verlag London 2013. P 30

smallest and least transparent of the five markets. [1]

In 2014, the global drilling and associated services market was worth $277 billion, 10% more than in 2013. Bearing in mind the sharp drop in drilling in 2015, the global market should fall this year by 27% and stand at around $200 billion.

The offshore drilling market fell by 11% but performed better than the onshore market (-28%). The offshore drilling market, worth $55 billion in 2015, was almost double the worth of the onshore market ($24 billion).

The most affected markets were well services, especially the fracking market, which fell by 38% over the year. Fracking and pumping operations, which account for 14% of the overall drilling market, had followed the rise in the development of shale gas in the United Stated and in 2015 they have generated turnover of around $27 billion. The tools, equipment and drilling products market rose in 2015 to $24 billion, i.e. a drop of 26% compared to 2014. The well completions, casings and services market has been more heavily affected, with a drop of 35% to $29 billion. The logging and

---

[1] Mark J.Kaiser, Brian F.Snyder: The Offshore Drilling Industry and Rig Construction in the Gulf of Mexico, Springer-Verlag London 2013. P 30: 31

directional drilling market has fallen by 29% to $26 billion. [1]

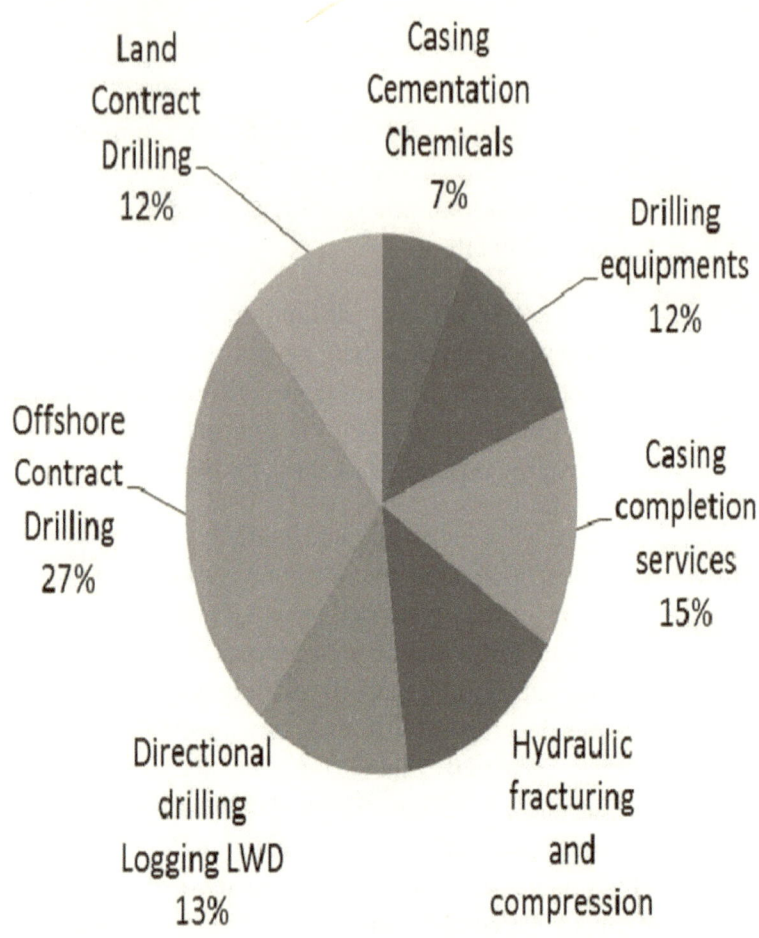

Turnover from onshore drilling operations alone increased by 3% in 2014 and

---

[1] Investments in exploration/production and refining 2015. IFP Energies Nouvelles - January 2016. P 17: 18

reached a record figure of $34 billion. With the drop-in drilling of unconventional reserves in the United States, the market fell in 2015 by 28% to amount to $24 billion. [1]

8 major groups hold 54% of the global drilling market and fourteen companies hold two thirds of the market. The sector leader is Nabors Industries, with a 12% share of the market, followed by Helmerich & Payne (10%). Eurasia Drilling is in third position (9%).

In 4th, 5th and 6th places are: Ensign, Precision Drilling and Patterson-UTI, all three with around a 5% market share. Saipem and Schlumberger, for which onshore drilling is not strictly their core business, are in 7th and 8th places respectively.

Among those companies with sharp falls in turnover in 2015 we find Ensign, Helmrich & Payne and Patterson-UTI with falls ranging from 30% to 40%. At the other end of the spectrum we find Eurasia Drilling and Ensign, faring better with falls limited to around -10%. 19

The value of the offshore drilling market alone is twice as large as the onshore drilling market. It grew in 2014 by 6%, reaching a record value of $62 billion. In 2015, the fall

---

[1]Investments in exploration/production and refining 2015. IFP Energies Nouvelles - January 2016. P 18

was around 11%, i.e. clearly less than for onshore drilling (-28%) and the market amounted to around $55 billion.

The offshore drilling market is also extremely concentrated since half is accounted for by 8 large groups and two thirds by 15 companies. In spite of sharp drop in turnover in 2015, the leading offshore drilling contractor is still Transocean, with 13% of the market share. Seadrill and ENSCO are still in 2nd and 3rd places respectively, each with around a 8% share of the market.

We find Noble Drilling, Diamond Offshore and COSL with between 4% and 5% of market share. The latter and Transocean have been badly affected in turnover terms in 2015. Rowan and Maersk, in 7th and 8th places, are among the rare companies increasing their turnover, with +11% and +14% respectively. [1]

---

[1] Investments in exploration/production and refining 2015. IFP Energies Nouvelles - January 2016. P 19

12. Contract Drilling Market

The contract drilling service market is described by day rates, utilization and fleet size. Day rates behave according to demand and supply conditions, and as regional demand approaches available supply, day rates generally rise. Demand for drilling is driven by the capital spending patterns of E&P companies, which in turn, is based on operator's expectations of future oil and gas prices, the availability of acreage, and many other factors. Day rates are an indicator of market conditions and the same drivers that impact day rates tend to influence the rest of the offshore service industry. [1]

Utilization is a system measure defined by the proportion of rigs working at a point in time to the available fleet within a specific region. Industry capacity is not a fixed resource because companies can add rigs through newbuilding and relocation to respond to higher demand and stack rigs when demand declines. While adding new capacity takes several years, rigs have very long lives (25+ years), and when demand weakens, overcapacity in the market may lead to prolonged declines in utilization. Stacking units removes capacity from the market and can be performed relatively quickly to help support prices, but stacking, like newbuilding

---

[1] Mark J.Kaiser, Brian F.Snyder: The Offshore Drilling Industry and Rig Construction in the Gulf of Mexico, Springer-Verlag London 2013. P 31

decisions, are firm specific and are not performed in unison. High utilization cause day rates to rise and provide a signal to operators that additional capacity can be absorbed in the market.

Fleet size describes the total number of rigs of a given water depth or class. Fleet size is described by firm, and when reported regionally, is an indicator of the total capacity in the drilling market at a given point in time. The scale and quality of a contractor's asset base is correlated with its revenue base. A large asset base implies a platform for sustainable earnings and cash flows and is related to a company's market position, its ability to compete in terms of cost structure, and the ability to obtain financing for capital projects. [1]

The number of offshore drilling companies varies over time, and in 2012 there were approximately 100 offshore drilling contractors and the market was dominated by a small number of firms, including Transocean, Ensco, Diamond Offshore and Seadrill. The top four firms owned 36 % of the 868 rigs in the world fleet circa 2011 and the top eight firms owned over half of the marketable rigs. Fleet size changes over time with changing market conditions, but the changes are often slow and

---

[1] Mark J.Kaiser, Brian F.Snyder: The Offshore Drilling Industry and Rig Construction in the Gulf of Mexico, Springer-Verlag London 2013. P 31

represent a small portion of the world's asset base. Asset transactions and additions are common but new firm entrants are infrequent. Most large firms are publicly owned and all but one of the major players in the market (National Drilling) are listed on stock exchanges. [1]

Distribution of rigs by class and operator circa 2Q2011

Company	Jackups	Semis	Drillships	Total	Ownership
Transocean	68	50	23	141	Public
Ensco	49	20	7	76	Public
Noble Drilling	45	14	13	72	Public
Hercules Offshore	53	0	0	53	Public
Diamond Offshore	13	32	3	48	Public
Seadrill	21	12	6	39	Public
COSL	27	6	0	33	State
Rowan	31	0	0	31	Public
Maersk Drilling	14	6	0	20	Subsidiary
Aban Offshore	15	0	3	18	Public
Saipem	7	7	2	16	Public
Nabors Offshore	16	0	0	16	Public
Atwood Oceanics	6	6	1	13	Public
National Drilling	13	0	0	13	State
ONGC	8	0	2	10	State
Petrobras	6	4	0	10	State
All others (87 firms)	147	66	46	259	
Top 4 firms	205	116	46	367	
Top 8 firms	337	134	52	523	
Total	539	223	106	868	

---

[1] Mark J.Kaiser, Brian F.Snyder: The Offshore Drilling Industry and Rig Construction in the Gulf of Mexico, Springer-Verlag London 2013. P 31: 32

In 2011, approximately 85 % of the active fleet was operating in the Persian Gulf, U.S. GOM, Brazil, North Sea, Southeast Asia, West Africa, India and China. Smaller markets include the Mexican GOM, Mediterranean, the Red Sea, Black Sea, Caspian Sea, the Caribbean and Australia. Frontier regions typically have less than five working rigs and include the Arctic Ocean, East Africa, Ghana, and the Philippines. [1]

Geographic distribution of active rigs by region in 2011

Region	Jackups	Semis	Drillships	Total
Persian Gulf	85	0	0	85
U.S. GOM	51	20	10	81
Brazil	3	52	15	70
North Sea	32	36	2	57
Southeast Asia	42	9	2	53
India	34	2	9	45
West Africa	17	13	9	39
China	28	4	0	32
Mexico	24	3	0	27
Egypt	20	2	2	24
All others	55	33	13	101
Top 4	171	108	27	306
Top 8	292	136	47	475
Total	394	175	57	626

---

[1] Mark J.Kaiser, Brian F.Snyder: The Offshore Drilling Industry and Rig Construction in the Gulf of Mexico, Springer-Verlag London 2013. P 33

12.1. Newbuild Market

The newbuild market is specified by deliveries and prices. The market is transparent because newbuilding is a significant capital expenditure for contractors and a significant source of revenue for rig-building shipyards. Prices are widely reported and tracked by the same firms that survey rig day rates.

Drilling contractors order rigs when the expected rate of return from operating a new rig exceeds company investment criteria. The benefit of investment depends on day rates and utilization over the life of the rig, and since these are unknown and uncertain, management employ their own expectations relative to their business strategy. The newbuild market is linked to conditions in the service market, and the cyclical nature of contract drilling causes similar cycles in the newbuild market. [1]

Prices in the newbuild market are a function of demand and shipyard labor, equipment and steel costs. As shipyard demand increases, backlogs develop and yards are able to command higher prices for services. In addition, demand at rig-building shipyards is generally associated with demand across the drilling supply chain. Therefore, demand and prices for

---

[1] Mark J.Kaiser, Brian F.Snyder: The Offshore Drilling Industry and Rig Construction in the Gulf of Mexico, Springer-Verlag London 2013. P 36

drilling equipment typically increase along with demand at shipyards, which leads to further price increases. [1]

Oil prices declined in the mid-1980s and demand collapsed, and during the decade 1986–1997, only 37 rigs were delivered. By the late 1990s, deep water drilling technology had advanced, but few rigs were capable of drilling in water depths greater than 1,500 ft. Contractors responded by upgrading and ordering a small number of floaters. New jackup orders also began in this period due to concerns about the age of the fleet and operator interest in more challenging reservoirs and harsh environments. [2]

2005, the number of jackup orders increased dramatically followed by an increase in floater orders, due in large part to increasing oil and gas prices and contractors expectations of future demand. Jackup deliveries peaked in 2009 with 38 rigs delivered, and floater deliveries peaked in 2011 with 52 units. In every year since 2000, high-spec jackup deliveries have outnumbered standard jackups, and in 2011

---

[1] Mark J.Kaiser, Brian F.Snyder: The Offshore Drilling Industry and Rig Construction in the Gulf of Mexico, Springer-Verlag London 2013. P 36
[2] Mark J.Kaiser, Brian F.Snyder: The Offshore Drilling Industry and Rig Construction in the Gulf of Mexico, Springer-Verlag London 2013. P 39

only three standard jackups were delivered compared to 33 high-spec rigs. [1]

12.2. Geographic Distribution

Contract drillers service oil and gas companies throughout the world wherever hydrocarbon resources are found or are believed to occur. The Persian Gulf, U.S. Gulf of Mexico, Brazil, the North Sea, Southeast Asia, and West Africa were the largest offshore markets in 2011 accounting for approximately 80 % of the supply with over 50 contracted rigs per region India and China were also significant markets with 77 contracted rigs. [2]

The U.S. GOM and North Sea were the first offshore regions to be explored, and production in the shallow water areas of these basins have been in decline for over a decade. New discoveries in the deep water GOM and Norwegian Continental Shelf have maintained capital investment, and both regions provide a stable and predictable business environment, a well-developed, reliable supply chain, and good geologic prospectivity.

---

[1] Mark J.Kaiser, Brian F.Snyder: The Offshore Drilling Industry and Rig Construction in the Gulf of Mexico, Springer-Verlag London 2013. P 40
[2] Mark J.Kaiser, Brian F.Snyder: The Offshore Drilling Industry and Rig Construction in the Gulf of Mexico, Springer-Verlag London 2013. P 52: 53

West African offshore markets are dominated by Nigeria and Angola. Investment and operation in West Africa is complicated by a tenuous security situation in Nigeria, limited infrastructure in Angola and Ghana, widespread corruption, and a lack of skilled labor throughout the region.

Southeast Asian markets are primarily composed of Indonesia and Malaysia, with Vietnam and the Philippines promising developing regions. The first offshore well in the region was drilled offshore Brunei territorial waters in 1958, and development intensified in the 1970s. Shallow water drilling dominates the region with significant midwater activity. Territorial disputes with China over the Spratley and Paracel Islands remain unresolved and have hindered capital investment in the region.

Brazil is a rapidly developing deep water market dominated by the state-owned oil company Petrobras. Brazil has made a concerted effort to increase the domestic content across the supply chain and in 2011 Petrobras announced that it will build 33 drillships in newly established Brazilian shipyards by 2020. [1]

The Persian Gulf is a shallow water market that has developed steadily over the last two decades. The region includes Saudi Arabia,

---

[1] Mark J.Kaiser, Brian F.Snyder: The Offshore Drilling Industry and Rig Construction in the Gulf of Mexico, Springer-Verlag London 2013. P 53

Qatar, the UAE, Iran, Kuwait, and Bahrain, and is dominated by National Oil Companies. The Persian Gulf includes Saudi Arabia's Safaniya field, the world's largest offshore oil field, and Qatar's North Field and adjacent South Pars field in Iran, the world's largest natural gas reservoir.

Mexico, India and China are mid-sized markets. India and China are developing markets with shallow and Deepwater sectors. Mexico is a mature region dominated by production at the shallow water Cantarell field. Cantarell peaked in 2004 and production declined by 70 % through 2011. Only 15 Deepwater wells were drilled in the Mexican GOM between 2004 and 2010. [1]

Smaller markets with less than 25 active rigs in 2011 include the Mediterranean Sea, Black Sea, Caspian Sea, Eastern Canada, the Caribbean and Western Australia. Frontier regions defined as having fewer than five rigs include the Arctic Ocean and East Africa, as well as previously unexplored regions such as

---

[1]Mark J.Kaiser, Brian F.Snyder: The Offshore Drilling Industry and Rig Construction in the Gulf of Mexico, Springer-Verlag London 2013. P 54

Ghana in West Africa and the Philippines in Southeast Asia. [1]

12.3. Contracts

Most drilling contracts are written on a day rate basis, but turnkey contracts are occasionally employed by small E&P companies with limited financial and technical expertise. In a turnkey well, the E&P company defines the well specifications (e.g., total depth and target, minimum hole size at total depth, formation evaluation requirements) and retains a turnkey company to plan and supervise the well on a lump-sum basis. The turnkey company retains a contractor under a day rate contract and holds the risk of cost overruns. [2]

Term contracts specify contract duration, whereas fixed well contracts specify the number of wells to be drilled. Term contracts are more common in most regions and markets, except in the U.S. GOM jackup market and Southeast Asia floater market where fixed well contracts dominate. Fixed well contracts are typically used for short term drilling programs while term contracts are used for longer exploration projects and field development.

---

[1] Mark J.Kaiser, Brian F.Snyder: The Offshore Drilling Industry and Rig Construction in the Gulf of Mexico, Springer-Verlag London 2013. P 54: 55
[2] Mark J.Kaiser, Brian F.Snyder: The Offshore Drilling Industry and Rig Construction in the Gulf of Mexico, Springer-Verlag London 2013. P 70

Worldwide, the average duration of fixed well contracts over the period 2000–2010 was 106 days, while the average for term contracts was 456 days.

In the U.S. GOM, jackups frequently work on a one-well basis and contractors have to find a new job at the completion of every well they drill. The average duration of jackup contracts in the U.S. GOM is significantly shorter than in other regions, but elsewhere deep water and shallow water rigs operate under similar contracts. [1]

Contractors generally seek a mix of long and short-term contracts to balance risk. Long-term contracts provide stable and durable cash flows, while short-term contracts provide upside exposure to improving markets and day rate upswings. Contracts were grouped by rig class and region into those greater than and less than the regional mean duration over the period 2000–2010. In every region and rig class, short-term contracts had lower day rates than long-term contracts. For jackups, the difference between contract types ranged from 13 % in Southeast Asia to 45 % in the Persian Gulf; for floaters, the premium was higher and ranged from 25 % to 85 %.

---

[1] Mark J.Kaiser, Brian F.Snyder: The Offshore Drilling Industry and Rig Construction in the Gulf of Mexico, Springer-Verlag London 2013. P 71

Contract duration premiums may vary temporally. If contractors expect future price and utilization to decline, they may accept lower day rates for long-term contracts. To control for the effects of time, the data were separated into three periods: 2000–2004, 2005–2008 and 2009–2010, corresponding roughly to stable, improving, and declining market conditions. Observed price changes are assumed to reflect market participant expectations. If the dayrate premium for long-term contracts depends on market conditions, there will be no premium for long-term contracts in the 2009–2010 period.

Separating the data into three-time periods, two rig classes and five regions provided 27 data sets for assessment. In 26 of 27 comparisons, longer-than-average contracts had higher day rates than shorter-than-average contracts, although the trend was only significant in 14 comparisons. There is no evidence that higher day rates for long-term contracts are affected by changing market conditions. [1]

12.4. Ownership

Drilling contractors are corporate entities that may be owned by investors or a government agency. Investor-owned drilling contractors may be publicly traded or privately

---

[1] Mark J.Kaiser, Brian F.Snyder: The Offshore Drilling Industry and Rig Construction in the Gulf of Mexico, Springer-Verlag London 2013. P 104

held. Publicly traded corporations have a large number of shareholders, whereas private firms are owned by a small number of shareholders and do not report financial or operational data. State-owned drilling contractors may be entirely owned by a state, or a fraction of the shares may be traded on a financial exchange. Ownership structure is important because it impacts business strategies, governance, access to debt and transparency.

12.4.1. Public Firms

The 14 largest publicly traded drilling contractors realized $26.4 billion in revenues in 2011 from an inventory of 501 drilling rigs (289 jackups, 148 semis, and 64 drillships) and generated more than half of the industry revenue Total fleet value is estimated at $107 billion, and collectively, the companies had an enterprise value of $111 billion. [1]

Transocean is the largest firm in terms of fleet size and revenue, and owned 141 rigs, or 16 % of the total fleet, including 22 % of the total floater fleet. In September 2012, Transocean agreed to sell 38 shallow water rigs to Shelf Drilling International Holdings Ltd for $1.05 billion as part of its strategy to unload older assets and focus on the high-end market.

---

[1] Mark J.Kaiser, Brian F.Snyder: The Offshore Drilling Industry and Rig Construction in the Gulf of Mexico, Springer-Verlag London 2013. P 77: 79

Seadrill, Diamond, Ensco and Noble are the next largest firms by fleet value and together own 209 rigs, including 88 floaters, and account for 24 % of the total fleet and 27 % of the floater fleet. Along with Transocean, these five firms are significantly larger than their nearest competitors and are categorized as "large-cap", while the nine smaller public firms are considered "mid-market" players.

All large cap firms except Seadrill are headquartered in the U.S., as are the mid–market firms Hercules, Rowan, Atwood and Vantage. Seadrill, Songa and Ocean Rig are headquartered in Norway. Most firms are incorporated in Switzerland, Cyprus, and the Cayman Islands for tax purposes. [1]

12.4.2. State-Owned Firms

China Oilfield Services Ltd (COSL) is the largest state-owned drilling contractor and owns as many rigs as UAE's National Drilling, India's Oil and Natural Gas Company (ONGC) and Brazil's Petrobras combined. In total, state owned firms own 127 drilling rigs, or about 15 % of the world fleet circa 2011. Most state-owned firms are jackup-oriented, but COSL, Petrobras and Socar own semisubmersibles and ONGC owns two drillships.

---

[1]Mark J.Kaiser, Brian F.Snyder: The Offshore Drilling Industry and Rig Construction in the Gulf of Mexico, Springer-Verlag London 2013. P 79

State-owned drilling contractors usually work exclusively in their home countries and are typically important players. They may be a subsidiary of a National Oil Company (e.g. COSL is owned by CNOOC) or the NOC may directly own and operate the drilling fleet. The largest state-owned drilling contractors are publicly traded firms in which the government is the majority shareholder; most other state-owned contractors are not publicly traded and are small players similar to small private firms. [1]

12.4.3. Private Firms

Private firms own about a third of the world's fleet and Deepwater rigs and play an important role in the floater markets in the North Sea and Brazil. Maersk Drilling, Stena Drilling, Dolphin, Schahin, and Odfjeld are the largest private contractors and controlled about 20 % of the private fleet circa 2011. Maersk Drilling is a subsidiary of A.P Moller-Maersk and Dolphin is a subsidiary of Fred Olsen Energy. The only privately held firm frequently operating in the U.S. GOM is Spartan Offshore, which is owned by a private equity firm and operates four low-spec jackups. About 50 firms own less than three

---

[1]Mark J.Kaiser, Brian F.Snyder: The Offshore Drilling Industry and Rig Construction in the Gulf of Mexico, Springer-Verlag London 2013. P 79

rigs and are either privately held or traded on the over the counter market. [1]

12.4.4. Market Share

The number of contracted days across all regional markets is used to measure market share. Over the decade 2000–2010, jackups were contracted between 250,000–350,000 days and floaters 150,000–275,000 days per year. Publicly traded firms dominate the market because of their larger fleet sizes, but state-owned contractors are important in the jackup market, constituting about 20% of days on contract, and in the floater market, private firms share of contracted days has historically ranged between 10 % to 20 %. [2]

12.5. Market Power

Large drilling contractors may be able to use market power to achieve higher day rates than their competitors. Transocean is the largest drilling contractor and was a market leader throughout the decade. The day rates received by Transocean were compared to its competitors in each region and rig class from 2000 to 2010. Transocean received higher than average day rates in the North Sea and U.S. GOM floater

---

[1] Mark J.Kaiser, Brian F.Snyder: The Offshore Drilling Industry and Rig Construction in the Gulf of Mexico, Springer-Verlag London 2013. P 79: 80

[2] Mark J.Kaiser, Brian F.Snyder: The Offshore Drilling Industry and Rig Construction in the Gulf of Mexico, Springer-Verlag London 2013. P 81

markets, however, when controlled for rig water depth, the day rate difference became non-significant. Similar results were obtained when the five largest drilling contractors (e.g. Transocean, Diamond, Noble, Ensco, and Seadrill) were evaluated as a group. Thus, while large drilling contractors receive higher day rates than their competitors in some regions and over some time periods, the effect appears to be due to the higher specifications of their fleets rather than the use of market power. [1]

12.6. RIG TIME LOSS AND NONPRODUCTIVE DRILLING TIME

The components of rig time loss, nonproductive drilling time, well design and drilling plan, and so on, are elaborated in this section, which would help the readers to comprehend the current problem and its context.

The decision to drill a well, especially exploratory well, requires diligent teamwork by geologist, geophysicist, petro physicist, drilling engineers, and others. The well design and drilling plan are prepared before the start of drilling and is normally followed till the completion of the well. It is a dynamic plan and might change depending on the borehole conditions encountered during drilling. A typical

---

[1]Mark J.Kaiser, Brian F.Snyder: The Offshore Drilling Industry and Rig Construction in the Gulf of Mexico, Springer-Verlag London 2013. P 106

well plan contains well location, target depth, water depth (for offshore), expected reservoir pressure, presence of hydrocarbon (oil/gas) and H2S, evaluation needs (i.e., mud log, well log, and core sample), phase-wise drilling plan, activity timeline, expected drilling problems, mitigation plan, and so on.

Drilling plan is prepared taking into account several factors, such as formation geology, pore pressure analysis, fracture gradient prediction, and so on, and contains casing design, cementing plan, drilling fluids plan, completion design, drill string design, drill bit program, identification of downhole complication and subsequent mitigation plan, well logging plan, well testing, coring plan, rig selection, and so on.

The selection of rig is generally guided by the principle of matching rig capacity with well depth, well type, and well size; in addition, rig availability is an influential factor for rig deployment. It specifically depends on the hook load capacity, deck space, blowout preventer (BOP) specification, drilling hydraulics requirement, drilling fluid maintenance and delivery system, water depth (for offshore), Health, Safety and Environment (HSE) requirement, and special rig requirement (i.e., desert rig, heli rig, small footprint rig, batch or pad drilling rig, etc.). Daily rig rentals and rig mobilization cost are also influential factors for rig selection.

Rig cycle time is the duration between rig release (from the current well) to rig release of the next well. Rig time comprises time for drilling, workover, logging, coring, production testing, rig move, and so on. Drilling time may be divided into productive and NPT.

Drilling, workover, and evaluation times are considered as productive rig time. Logging, coring, and production testing time are known as evaluation time. *The components of nonproductive drilling time are stuck pipe (drill string or tool), fishing, lost circulation, well control, wiper trips related to wellbore instability, pipe failure, equipment failure, downhole complications, WoM and tools, waiting on weather (WoW) (especially for offshore), waiting on decision (WoD), and so on.* NPT has both reducible and irreducible components. While some activities such as WoW, and so on, are unavoidable, many others can be avoided or controlled to a great extent. *This study tries to identify the root causes of this controllable rig time loss and suggests measures to optimize these.*

Geologic formation (i.e., hardness and composition of rock, formation pressure, temperature, behavior, etc.) and characteristics of well (i.e., well type, location and depth of target reservoir, etc.) have a casting influence on NPT. It is observed that NPT is generally higher in hard, abrasive, and heterogeneous formation, which is prone to drill string failures. It is also noted that deep reservoir is generally associated with high pressure and high temperature, hydrogen sulfide (H2S) and carbon dioxide (CO2) contamination, and prone to downhole complication. The well trajectory, drilling fluid characteristics, and hydraulics have important role in mitigating downhole complications, and thereby minimize nonproductive drilling time. Drilling plan recognizes these complexities, and appropriate measures are required to optimize nonproductive drilling time. [1]

---

[1] Sanjib Chowdhury: Optimization and Business Improvement Studies in Upstream Oil and Gas Industry. John Wiley & Sons, Inc. 2016. P 38:39

13. BOREHOLE LOGGING

Another valuable exploration method is geophysical borehole logging, which involves drilling a well and the use of instruments to log or make measurements at various levels in the hole by such means as electrical resistivity, radioactivity, acoustics, or density. In addition, formation samples (cores) are taken for physical and chemical tests.

The use of electrical logging is based on the fact that the resistivity of a rock layer is a function of its fluid content. Oil-filled sand has very high resistivity. The method consists of passing a current between an electrode at the surface and one that is lowered into the hole, the latter being uncased and filled with drilling mud. Any change in the resistivity conditions around the moving electrode affects the flow of current and voltage distribution around it.

Voltage fluctuations can be measured by a pair of separate electrodes used in conjunction with the moving electrode.

The natural radioactive properties of many constituents of rock have made it possible to develop and use nuclear radiation detectors (radioactive logging) in the borehole or even in holes that have already been cased. Two commonly used methods are g-ray and neutron logging. In the first case, the natural radiation from the rock is used. In the second, a neutron source is employed to excite the release of radiation from the rock. The neutron source is usually a mixture of beryllium and radium, but it can be a miniature Van der Graaff particle accelerator. The neutron method is a means for determining the relative porosity or rock formations; the ¥-ray log helps define shale.

The acoustic logging method is quite similar to surface seismic work. Instead of explosives, an electrically operated acoustic pulse generator is used. In one instrument, the generator is separated from the receiver by an acoustic insulator. The design permits automatic selection and recording of the travel times of the onsets of pulses that travel through the rock wall of the hole as the instrument moves down or up. Signals are recorded continuously at the surface, being transmitted through a cable on which the instrument is suspended. The velocity log provided by the instrument helps to define beds and evaluate formation porosity.

Density can now be logged with a new technique that uses radioactivity (density logging).

The instrument consists of a radioactive cobalt source of ¥-rays and a Geiger counter as a detector, which is shielded from the source. The rock formation is bombarded with the ¥-rays, some of which are scattered back from the formation and enter the detector. The degree to which the original radiation is adsorbed is a function of the density of the rock.

Test well sampling is another important method used in the search for oil (core sampling).

Well data obtained from the examination of formation samples taken from various depths in the borehole are of considerable value in deciding further exploratory work. These samples can be cores, which have been taken from the hole by a special coring device or drill cuttings screened from the circulating drilling mud. The major purpose of sample examination is to identify the various strata in the borehole and compare their positions with the standard stratigraphic sequence of all the sedimentary rocks occurring in the specific basin where the hole has been drilled. [1]

---

[1] James G. Speight: The Chemistry and Technology of Petroleum. FOURTH EDITION. Taylor & Francis Group, LLC. 2007. P 139:140

14. Logging/measurement while drilling (LWD/MWD)

Basic MWD technology was first introduced in the 1980s by drilling companies and was initially restricted to retrievable inserts for directional measurements and then natural GR logs. These developments were quickly followed by logging tools integrated into drill collars (DCs) (LWD). Recently, LWD development has progressed to the stage where most of the conventional wireline logging tools can be effectively replaced by a LWD equivalent. Early LWD technology was often considered to be inferior to wireline. However, recent mergers between wireline and drilling companies has resulted in technology-transfer in R&D which has led to a significant improvement in LWD log quality. A lazy use of terminology within the industry means that LWD and MWD can be considered as synonymous. A more appropriate term for today's sophisticated devices is formation evaluation while drilling (FEWD).

Perhaps the greatest stimulus for the development of such tools has been the proliferation of high-angle wells in which deviation surveys are difficult and wireline logging services are impossible (without some sort of pipe conveyance system), and where LWD logging can minimize formation damage by reducing open hole exposure times.

Whilst providing deviation and logging options in high-angle wells is a considerable benefit, the greatest advantage offered by LWD technology, in either conventional or high-angle wells, is the acquisition of real time data at surface. Most of the LWD applications which are now considered standard, exploit this feature in some way, and include

_ real time correlation for picking coring and casing points

_ real time overpressure detection in exploration wells

_ real time logging to minimize 'out of target' sections (geosteering)

_ real time formation evaluation to facilitate 'stop drilling' decisions.

Although there are a wide range of LWD services available, not all are required in every situation and the full LWD logging suites which include directional and formation logging sensors are run much less frequently than gamma/resistivity/ directional combinations. An example of an LWD tool configuration is given in the Figure.

All LWD tools have both a power supply and data transmission system, often combined in one purpose-built collar and usually located above the measurement sensors as shown in the Figure (a Baker–Hughes multicombination tool).

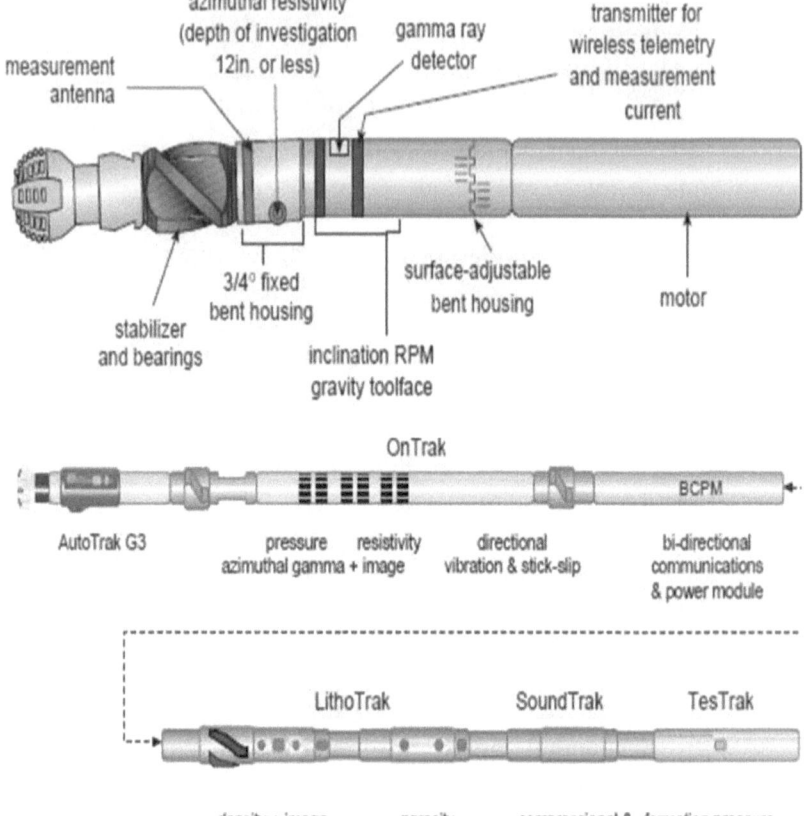

Data transmission may be within the downhole assembly from the sensors to a memory device or from the sensors to surface. The latter is usually achieved by mud pulse telemetry, a method by which data are transmitted from the tool in real time, that is as data are being acquired. Positive or negative pressure pulses created in the mud stream downhole travel through the mud (inside the drill pipe) to surface and are detected by a pressure transducer in the flowline. Positive pressure pulses are created by extending a plunger into a choke orifice, momentarily restricting flow, an operation which is repeated to create a binary data string. Negative pulses are created by opening a bypass valve and venting mud to the annulus, momentarily reducing the drill pipe pressure.

Data transmission rate per foot is a function of both pulse frequency and ROP. Sensors acquire and transmit data samples at fixed time intervals and therefore the sampling per foot is a function of ROP. Current tools allow a real time sampling and transmission rate similar to wireline tools as long as the penetration rate does not exceed about 100 ft/h. If drilling progresses faster or if there are significant variations in penetration rate, resampling by depth as opposed to time intervals may be required. The quantity of data that can be transmitted in real time is limited and focused towards responses used for geosteering and other drilling decisions. A full data set is stored in the downhole memory which is retrieved when the tool is brought to the surface.

Electrical power is supplied to LWD tools either from batteries run in the downhole assembly or from an alternator coupled to a turbine set in the mud stream.

In terms of log data quality and tool response modern LWD/FEWD tools can be as good as their wireline counterparts. However, the biggest issue when comparing the two technologies is depth control. Wireline depth is accurately measured at the surface by a spooling wheel in front of the cable drum which records the length of cable that has been reeled in. LWD depth is measured as 'drillers depth' where the driller records the length of drill pipe that has been run in the hole. Individual lengths of pipe can differ and the 'pipe tally' (record of pipe length) is not always accurate. Additionally, the actual length of pipe in a long borehole may change depending upon the amount of compression or tension within the string. On occasions when LWD and wireline logs over the same section are compared, the depth differences can be up to several meters. Currently, LWD companies are designing depth-adjustment software to overcome this problem.
[1]

---

[1]Frank Jahn, Mark Cook and Mark Graham: HYDROCARBON EXPLORATION AND PRODUCTION. 2ND EDITION. Elsevier B.V. 2008. P 149: 151

14.1. Origination of Well Logging

Well logging, as a terminology, is originated from France in 1927. Its primary meaning is electrical coring, which is a continuous record of characteristics of rock formations traversed by a measurement device in the well bore. Well logging, however, means different things for different people. For a geologist, it is primarily a mapping technique for exploring the surface. For a petro physicist, it is a means to evaluate the hydrocarbon production potential of a reservoir. For a geophysicist, it is a source of complementary data for surface seismic analysis. For a reservoir engineer, it may simply supply values for use in a simulation.

The initial uses of well logging were for correlating similar patterns of electrical conductivity from one well to another, sometimes over large distance. As the measuring techniques improved and multiplied, applications began to be directed to the quantitative evaluation of hydrocarbon-bearing formations. Much of the following text is directed toward the understanding of the measurement devices and interpretation techniques developed for this type of formation evaluation.

Although well logging grew from the special need of the petroleum industry to evaluate hydrocarbon accumulations, it is relevant to a number of other areas of interest to earth scientists. A detailed analysis of measurement principles precedes the discussion of these applications. In this process, well logging is seen to require the synthesis of a number of diverse physical sciences: physics, chemistry, electrochemistry, geochemistry, acoustics, nuclear, and geology.

14.2. What Is Well Logging?

Well logging is the process of continuous recording various physical, chemical, electrical, or other properties of the rock or fluid mixtures penetrated by drilling a well into the earth's mantle. Logging also includes control of boreholes for technical condition, formation sampling, and sidewall coring. The process of logging involves a number of elements, which are schematically illustrated in. [1]

The continuous recording of a geophysical parameter along a borehole produces a geophysical log. The value of the measurement is plotted continuously against depth in the well. For example, the resistivity log is a continuous plot of a formation's resistivity from the bottom to the top of the well and may represent over thousands of meters.

The most appropriate name of this continuous depth-related record is a wireline

---

[1] Hongqi Liu: Principles and Applications of Well Logging, Petroleum Industry Press, china 2017. P 1: 2

geophysical well log, conveniently shortened to well log or log. It has often been called an "electrical log" because historically the first logs were electrical measurements of electrical properties. However, the measurements are no longer simply electrical, and modern methods of data transmission do not necessarily need a wireline so the name above is recommended.

In its most usual form, an oil well log is a record displayed on a graph, with the measured physical property of the rock on one axis and depth (distance from the surface) on the other axis. More than one property may be displayed on the same graph. Some of the properties that can be measured are the following: [1]

(1) the self(spontaneous) potential of rock/borehole fluid interface

(2) the resistivity of the rock at various distances from the borehole

(3) the acoustic travel time of the rock

(4) the neutron absorption cross-section

(5) the electron density of the rock

(6) the size of the borehole drilled in the rock

---

[1] Hongqi Liu: Principles and Applications of Well Logging, Petroleum Industry Press, china 2017. P 2: 3

(7) the flow rate and density of fluids in the well bore

(8) numerous other related or derived properties of the rock and well bore environment.

14.3. Use of Logs

Well logging, from its origination about 100 years ago, has been proofed an utmost useful technology both in exploration and exploitation. Its measurements occupy a central position in the whole life of a well. The traditional role of well logging lies in two domains: formation comprehensive evaluation and completion evaluation. For the first part, it can be summarized in four key questions of primary phase: [1]

(1) Are there any hydrocarbons, and if so are they oil or gas?

(2) Where are the hydrocarbons?

(3) How much hydrocarbon was contained in the formation?

(4) How producible are the hydrocarbons?

In fact, all questions will come down to this one practical concern, which is just the most difficult one to answer. The reason is a most important parameter, permeability of the

---

[1] Hongqi Liu: Principles and Applications of Well Logging, Petroleum Industry Press, china 2017. P 7: 8

formation, which is the most uncertainty one. Many empirical methods are used to extract permeability from logging with varying degrees of success.

The second domain of well logging is completion evaluation, which consist of a diverse group of logging tools, such as cement bond quality logging, stability of borehole wall, flow rate, density of the fluid in pipe, temperature, and pressure in pipe or formation. If a field went into late life, many pay zones will be flooded by injected water or original formation water. Production engineer concerned how much degree of the water-flooded? What about the saturation of residual oil? How long will a well sustain production? All of these above questions can be solved completely or in some degree by well logging technology. [1]

14.4. Production Logging

Production logging traditionally encompasses a number of well logging techniques that run on completed injection or production wells, with the goal to evaluate the well itself or the reservoir performance. In recent years, however, the role of production logging has expanded to include applications that start at the early stages of drilling and that last throughout the life of the well. The purpose of

---

[1]Hongqi Liu: Principles and Applications of Well Logging, Petroleum Industry Press, china 2017. p 8

production logs is to evaluate fluid flow inside and outside pipe or, in some cases, to evaluate the well completion directly. The most common application of production logging is the measurement of the well's flow profile, the distribution of flow into or out of the well-bore. Wade et al., referring to production wells, state that production logging is used to answer the question "How much of what fluid is coming from where."

The primary logging methods that will be considered are temperature, radioactive-tracer, and spinner-flowmeter logs for single-phase flow; temperature, fluid-density, fluid-capacitance, and flowmeter logs in multiphase flow; and noise, cement-bond logs as applied for well completion evaluation.

Major Applications of Production Logging Include: [1]

(1) evaluating completion efficiency

(2) detecting mechanical problems, breakthrough, coning

(3) providing guidance for workovers, enhanced recovery projects

(4) monitoring and profiling of production and injection

---

[1] Hongqi Liu: Principles and Applications of Well Logging, Petroleum Industry Press, china 2017. p 181

(5) detecting thief zones, channeled cement

(6) single layer and multiple layer well test evaluation

(7) determining reservoir characteristics

(8) identifying reservoir boundaries for field development.

A family of production logging tools, designed specifically for measuring the performance of producing and injection wells, is available. The sensors now included are: [1]

(1) thermometer

(2) fluid-density (manometer, nuclear)

(3) hold up meter

(4) flowmeter spinners (continuous, full borehole, diverter)

(5) Manometer (strain gauge, quartz gauge)

(6) caliper

(7) noise (single frequency, multiple frequency)

(8) radioactive tracer.

---

[1] Hongqi Liu: Principles and Applications of Well Logging, Petroleum Industry Press, china 2017. P 182

15. The Advanced Well Logging Technology

15.1. Eclips-5700 Well Logging System

Baker Hughes Inc. is a leader in oilfield services in the world. Baker Atlas is a subsidiary company of Baker Hughes. Baker Atlas offers a complete range of downhole well logging services for every environment, including advanced formation evaluation, production and reservoir engineering, petrophysical, and geophysical data acquisition services. ECLIPS-5700 well logging system, which is manufactured by Baker Atlas, is a set of advanced system in the world. [1]

ECLIPS is the abbreviation of Enhanced Computer Logging Interpretation Processing System. ECLIPS-5700 well logging system can provide data acquisition and processing of the conventional logging and the imaging logging. Menu drive and "help" function is introduced into ECLIPS-5700 well logging system, which is convenient for operation. ECLIPS can offer abroad diagnostic program, for example the diagnostic program of Power and Telemetry system and the diagnostic program selected by the user. ECLIPS can monitor the quality of the well logging by the

---

[1] Hongqi Liu: Principles and Applications of Well Logging, Petroleum Industry Press, china 2017. p 271

real-time display of curve and data processing.
(1)

In logging the well, ECLIPS-5700 well logging system uses four main types of equipment: the downhole instrument (which measures the data), the computerized surface data acquisition system (to store and analyze the data), the cable or wireline (which serves as both mechanical and data communication link with the downhole instruments), and the hoisting equipment to raise and lower the instruments. In this unit, we will mainly introduce the downhole instrument. We will introduce the conventional logging instrument in this passage, and we will introduce the imaging logging instrument in the next passage.

15.2. Excell-2000 Well Logging System

Halliburton developed the Excell 2000 logging system, a state-of-the-art integrated logging platform that consistently delivers accurate, high-quality data, and provides powerful post-processing workstation capabilities. The system enables greatly improved wellsite performance and provides a standard platform from which new logging tools and software currently in development can be more efficiently operated. And the most important, it allows critical formation data to be

---

(1)Hongqi Liu: Principles and Applications of Well Logging, Petroleum Industry Press, china 2017. p 271: 272

at the right place, at the right time to help ensure correct decisions are made about your well.

The Excell 2000 is a new-generation logging system. This platform unites a family of data acquisition systems to provide a broad spectrum of real-time geophysical data acquisition system. Systems can be optimized based on the services required at each site. Each configuration uses the same operator interface, thus providing the same "look and feel" to each system. [1]

---

[1] Hongqi Liu: Principles and Applications of Well Logging, Petroleum Industry Press, china 2017. p 275

16. Integrated Interpretation of Well Logging Data

Well logging, has become in some ways the geologist's eye—an eye that is imperfect and sometimes distorted but nevertheless not blind—and an instrument for the reservoir engineer, occupies a special place and plays an important role in petroleum research by the economies that they bring and the amount of information they contain.

Integrated interpretation of well logging, as applied to subsurface petroleum reservoirs, has historically been defined as the practice of determining reservoir thickness, lithology, porosity, hydrocarbon saturation, and permeability, using information obtained from a borehole. This definition probably represents a consensus, which is a summary of quotations on the definition, scope, and objectives of formation evaluation from experts on the subjects.

The evaluation of a series of reservoirs based on well log data has the following essential objectives: [1]

(a) Location of reservoirs, vertically within the drilled section, and spatially by determining the

---

[1] Hongqi Liu: Principles and Applications of Well Logging, Petroleum Industry Press, china 2017. p 289: 290

x, y, and z coordinates for the upper and lower boundaries of each reservoirs.

(b) Determination of fluid type within the reservoir: types of possible hydrocarbons, gas, oil, or bitumen; salt content of the formation water.

(c) Calculation of reserves, both moveable and in place. This involves: determination of both the apparent and the actual thickness of each reservoir from dip meter data;

computation of the petrophysical parameters, i.e., porosity (total, primary, secondary and effective) and mode of distribution of the porosity and geometry of the pores;

• computation of water and oil saturation;

• calculation of pay thickness;

• selection of cut-offs;

• determination of reservoir the productivity.

determination of the productivity of the well, that is maximum output for

optimal recovery of the hydrocarbons in place. This involves:

determination of mobility;

calculation of the total and relative permeability;

determination of the formation pressure.

(e) Determination of the lithology, facies, and depositional environment so as to get an idea of the lateral extent of the petrophysical features of the reservoir: exact nature of principal minerals and, if possible, of the accessory ones, since any error in mineral type can lead to significant errors in the calculation of porosity, of saturation and of reservoir:

percentages of the principal minerals;

clay content, clay type and distribution;

estimation of texture, grain size distribution, sorting, and grain shape.

17. Mud Logging

Very often the drilling system will include on-site mud logging equipment and personnel and even digital computer facilities. Such have become a standard feature of drilling operations in many parts of the world, especially in deep wells, offshore locations, remote wildcats, and in areas where special and potentially dangerous drilling conditions may be encountered. Most drilling rigs today are provided with various devices that automatically record such parameters as weight of the drill string, mud pump pressure, rate of penetration, mud pit fluid level, mud flow rate, etc., all as functions of time.

Facilities such as these serve not only to monitor the overall progress of the drilling operation, but also permit the prediction and rapid assessment of potentially dangerous situations. With the data obtained, calculations can be made to insure a safer and more efficient drilling operation. [1]

Hydrocarbon well logging, better known as mud logging, is a service performed at the rig site with a self-contained mobile field laboratory. These mud logging units are equipped to provide a variety of services, depending upon the requirements of the well, but

---

[1] Ellis H. Austin: Drilling Engineering, International Human Resources Development Corporation • Boston D. Reidel Publishing Company, 1983. P 122

the two basic services are (1) detection of hydrocarbons in the drilling mud and drill cuttings, and (2) monitoring of the drilling mud density. The former is, of course, primarily for the detection of hydrocarbon-bearing strata while the latter is primarily for blowout prevention. [1]

Modern mud logging units are capable of providing a variety of additional tests and services applicable to essentially all areas of the drilling operation and particularly to the functions of the well site geologist. These tests and services are associated with measurements and interpretations of drilling mud and well cuttings data and the monitoring of various aspects of the drilling operation.

The mud-logging unit is generally powered by the rig's electrical generator and is connected to the rig in three ways: (1) by a hose-and-pump connection to the mud-return flow line; (2) by cables to moving rig components; and (3) by electrical lines to sensors or recording devices.

Formation evaluation for the determination of commercial oil and gas potential requires knowledge of porosity, pay zone thickness (net pay), and fluid saturation

---

[1] Ellis H.Austin: Drilling Engineering, International Human Resources Development Corporation • Boston D. Reidel Publishing Company, 1983. P 122: 123

distribution. It is also often helpful to determine some quantitative index indicating the presence of hydrocarbon and whether such hydrocarbon is producible in commercial quantities (movable oil index). Three types of porosity logs (sonic, density, and neutron) are available, and while all porosity logs are primarily responsive to porosity, other formation characteristics also influence the measurements. Each device responds differently to the effects of rock lithology and type and quantity of the fluids (water, oil, gas) in the pore space. Thus, a combination of two or three porosity logs may often yield a better understanding of porosity, lithology, and pore geometry.

In clean, highly porous, and permeable formation, sonic, formation density, and neutron tools all give sufficiently accurate porosity values. For shaley sand, the formation density log appears to provide the best value of porosity.
[1]

Of the formation parameters obtained directly from logs, resistivity is of particular importance. Resistivity measurements, with porosity and water resistivity, are used to obtain water saturation. Water saturation values may be computed by various methods such as (I) the Archie method, (2) the ratio method, (3) the

---

[1] MIHIR K. SINHA, LARRY R. PADGETT: RESERVOIR ENGINEERING TECHNIQUES USING FORTRAN. D. Reidel Publishing Company 1985. P 19

shaley sand method, (4) the two-porosity method, and (5) the three-porosity method.

A clean sand made up of large-to-medium-sized grain and containing hydrocarbon in the intergranular porosity shows a high degree of resistivity in comparison to nearby water sand. For such sand, the Archie inethod provides a reasonable estimate of water saturation. The ratio method of water saturation determination provides a verification and an improvement to the values generated by the Archie method.

However, often all three porosity logs may not become available for such formation. In such a situation, two-porosity (density and neutron) logs may be used for the analysis for water saturation with somewhat decreased reliability. [1]

Eventually, only the drilling of an exploration well will prove the validity of the concept. A 'wildcat' well is drilled in a region with no prior well control. Wells either result in discoveries of oil and gas, or they find the objective zone to be water-bearing in which case they are termed 'dry'.

Exploration activities are potentially damaging to the environment. The cutting down

---

[1] MIHIR K. SINHA, LARRY R. PADGETT: RESERVOIR ENGINEERING TECHNIQUES USING FORTRAN. D. Reidel Publishing Company 1985. P 19: 20

of trees in preparation for an onshore seismic survey may result in severe soil erosion in years to come. Offshore, fragile ecological systems such as reefs can be permanently damaged by spills of crude or mud chemicals. Responsible companies will therefore carry out an environmental impact assessment (EIA) prior to activity planning and draw up contingency plans should an accident occur. [1]

---

[1]Frank Jahn, Mark Cook and Mark Graham: HYDROCARBON EXPLORATION AND PRODUCTION. 2ND EDITION. Elsevier B.V. 2008. P 25

18. Well correlation

Well correlation is used to establish and visualize the lateral extent and the variations of reservoir parameters. In carrying out a correlation we subdivide the objective sequence into lithologic units and follow those units or their generic equivalent laterally through the area of interest. As we have seen earlier, the reservoir parameters such as N/G, porosity, permeability, etc. are to a large extent controlled by the reservoir geology, in particular the depositional environment. Thus, by correlation we can establish lateral and vertical trends of those parameters throughout the structure. This will enable us to calculate hydrocarbon volumes in different parts of a field, predict production rates and optimize the location for appraisal and development wells.

Usually well logs are only one type of data used to establish a correlation. Any meaningful interpretation will need to be supported by paleontological data (micro fossils) and palynological data (pollen of plants). The logs most frequently for correlation are GR, density logs, sonic log, dip meter and formation imaging tools. On a detailed scale, these curves should always be calibrated with core data as described below.

On a larger scale, for example in a regional context, seismic stratigraphy will help to establish a reliable correlation. It is employed in combination with the concept of sequence stratigraphy. This technique, initially introduced by Exxon Research, and since then considerably refined, postulates that global (eustatic) sea level changes create unconformities which can be used to subdivide the stratigraphic record. These unconformities are modified and affected by more local (relative) changes in sea level as a result of local tectonic movements, climate and the resulting impact on sediment supply. The most significant stratigraphic discontinuities used in a sequence stratigraphic approach are

_ regressive surfaces of erosion, caused by a lowering of sea level

_ transgressive surfaces of erosion, caused by an increase in sea level

_ maximum flooding surfaces at times of 'highest' sea level.

Relative sea level changes affect many shallow marine and coastal depositional environments.

Sequence stratigraphy integrates information gleaned from seismic, cores, well logs and often outcrops. In many cases, it has increased the understanding of reservoir geometry and heterogeneity and improved the correlation of individual drainage units. Sequence stratigraphy has also proved a powerful tool to predict presence and regional distribution of reservoirs. For instance, shallow marine regressive surfaces may indicate the presence of turbidites in a nearby, deeper marine area.

In preparation for a field wide 'quick look' correlation, all well logs need to be corrected for borehole inclination. This is done routinely with software which uses the measured depth (MD) below the derrick floor ('along hole depth' below derrick floor [AHBDF] or MD) and the acquired directional surveys to calculate the true vertical depth subsea (TVSS). This is the vertical distance of a point below a common reference level, for instance chart datum (CD) or MSL. The Figure shows the relationship between the different depth measurements.

To start the correlation process, we take the set of logs and select a datum plane. This is a marker which can be traced through all data points. A good datum plane would be a continuous shale because we can assume that it represents a 'flooding surface' present over a wide area. Since shales are low-energy deposits, we may also assume that they have been deposited mostly horizontally, blanketing the underlying sediments thus 'creating' a true datum plane.

Next, we align all logs at the datum plane which now becomes a straight horizontal line. Note that by doing so we ignore all structural movements to which the sequence has been exposed.

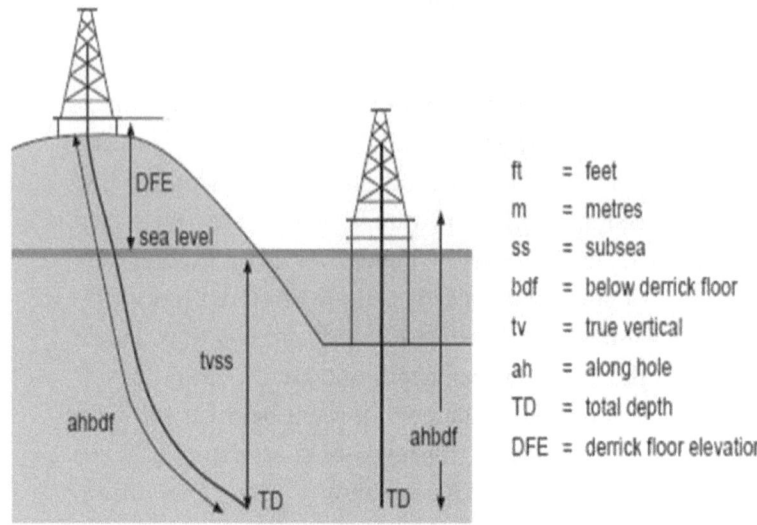

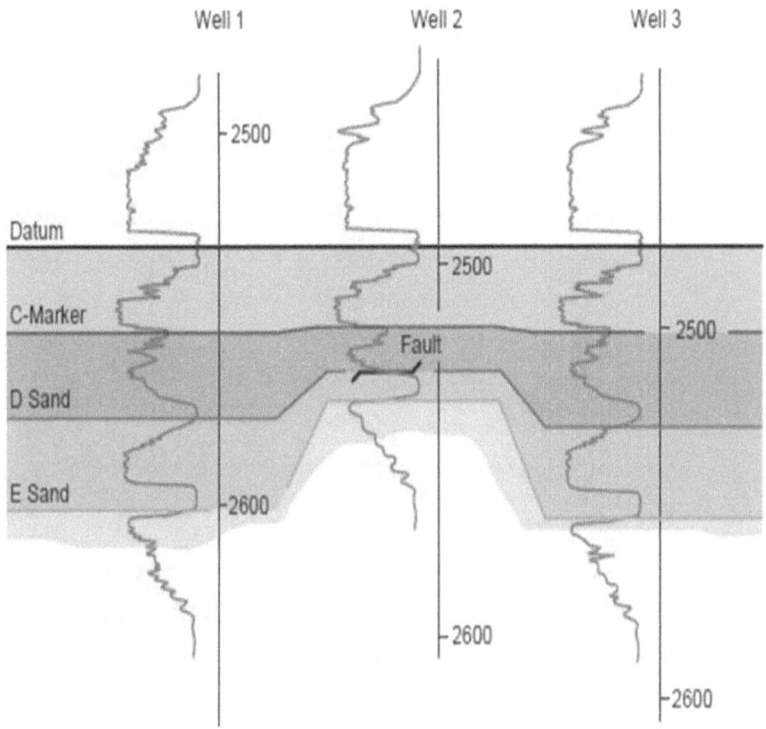

We can now correlate all 'events' below or above the datum plane by comparing the log response. In many instances, correlations are ambiguous. Where two or more correlation options seem possible, the problem may be resolved by checking whether an interpretation is consistent with the geological model and by further validating it with other data. This could be, for instance, pressure data which will indicate whether or not sands in different wells communicate. In cases where correlation is difficult to establish, a detailed paleontological zonation may be useful.

If correlation is 'lost', that is if no similarity exists any more between the log shapes of two wells, this could be for a number of reasons:

_ faulting: the well has intersected a fault and part of the sequence is missing.

Faulting can also cause a duplication of sequences!

_ unconformity: parts of the sequence have been eroded.

These events will need to be marked on the correlation panel. In case of faults, the thickness of the missing section or 'cut out' should be quantified.

Correlations on paper panels are made easier if a type log has been created of a typical and complete sequence of the area. If this log is available as a transparency, it can be easily compared against the underlying paper copy. Type logs are also handy if the reservoir development has to be documented in reports or presentations.

To make the correlation results applicable for the field development process, it may be desirable to display the correlated units in their true structural position. For instance, if water injection is planned for the field, water should enter the structure

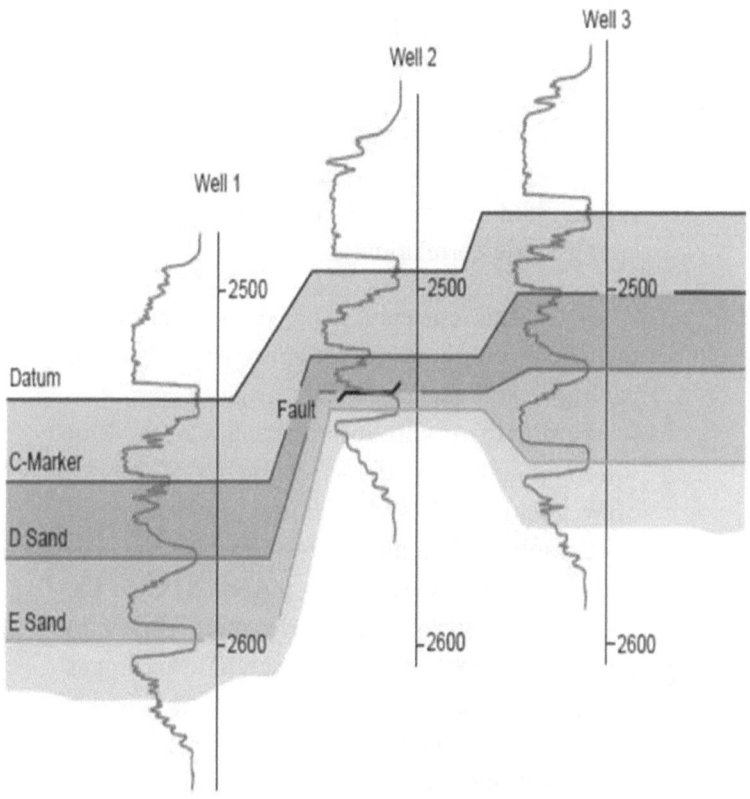

at or below the OWC and move upwards. Hence the correlation panel should visually show the sand development in the same direction. For this, all markers on the panel are displayed and connected at their TVSS position. This is called a structural correlation.

If appropriate, correlation panels may contain additional information such as depositional environments, porosities and permeabilities, saturations, lithological descriptions and indications of which intervals have been cored. [1]

Ten stratigraphic bounding surfaces (five SBs and five intervening MFSs) recognized in this study were used for well log sequence stratigraphic correlations.

This correlation aided in determining the lateral continuity or discontinuity of stratal packages and facies geometry. The occurrence of the identified chronostratigraphic surfaces at different depths in dip direction (N–S, NNE–SSW and NE–SW) shows evidence of stratigraphic thickening down dip (southwards) and tinning, up-dip (northwards). In the correlation along strike (E–W), there appear to be variable thickness in stratigraphic packages across the fields. The flattening at various stratigraphic bounding MFS(s) indicates a shift of depositional center from the northern to the southern section of the study area. [2]

---

[1] Frank Jahn, Mark Cook and Mark Graham: HYDROCARBON EXPLORATION AND PRODUCTION. 2ND EDITION. Elsevier B.V. 2008. P 153: 156

[2] Chidozie Izuchukwu Princeton Dim: Hydrocarbon Prospectivity in the Eastern Coastal Swamp Depo-belt of the Niger Delta Basin. 2017. P 36: 39

19. Producing the Well

Producing the well means bringing the fluids that flowed from the formation into the borehole from the bottom of the well to the surface. Fluids need to be brought to the surface at the desired rate and with sufficient pressure to flow through the surface-treating facilities. Some reservoirs possess such a high pressure that it can produce the desired rates at high bottom-hole pressures that could push the fluids to the surface at the desired wellhead pressure. This mode of production is known as natural flow. Reservoirs with high initial pressures and with strong pressure support (i.e., from bottom water) can be produced under natural flow for extended periods of time.

When the reservoir pressure declines, pressure support may be provided by injecting water or gas into the reservoir to maintain natural flow at desired rates and surface pressures. In some cases, however, pressure support may not be sufficient to maintain desired natural flow. This usually occurs due to increased water production, which increases the hydrostatic head and friction losses in the tubing. Therefore, the fluids may reach the surface at lower than desired pressures or may not even reach the surface. In such cases, external means of lifting the fluids to the surface will be needed. These means are known as the artificial lift methods. Production engineers are responsible

225

for selecting, designing, installing, and operating artificial lifting facilities. [1]

20. The Role of Drilled Wells in Development

All the activity described above for oil exploration leads only to an evaluation of the probability that oil is in a particular location. Once it seems probable that there really is oil, wells must be drilled. Reservoirs and oil fields are discovered only by drilling to sufficient depths to verify what was recommended by an exploration team. Wildcat wells, exploratory wells, or test wells are drilled first for probing purposes. An unsuccessful wildcat well is called a *dry hole*. A successful wildcat well is called a *discovery well*. Subsequent wells drilled into proven reservoirs for production purposes are called *development wells*. The drilling of test wells is the costliest single operation in oil exploration.

One exploratory well alone does not indicate extensive oil accumulation. Other wells, carefully located near the well where oil has been discovered, are drilled to discover if there is a reservoir in the area and approximately how much is available and can be recovered. To do this, first reliable information must be obtained

---

[1]Hussein K. Abdel-Aal Mohamed A. Aggour Mohamed A. Fahim: Petroleum and Gas Field Processing. Second Edition. Taylor & Francis Group, LLC. 2016. P 37

as to the quantity of oil (and gas) that is recoverable, so an economic and proper size and type of surface crude oil production plant can be set up.

Second, the characteristics of the oil itself and the nature and amount of oil in the reservoir should be determined from the samples of the reservoir. The raising of oil to the ground surface and then the handling of the oil at ground surface will depend to a great extent on the nature of the oil itself and its associated gas. Crude oil can range from very heavy viscous oil, almost a tar, with little or no gas dissolved in it and under very low pressure, to an extremely light, straw-colored oil with a considerable volume of gas, known as a condensate-type crude. The condensate-type crude is more likely to be found at great depths. Under conditions of high pressure and temperature that exist at deep levels, the crude is usually in the gaseous stage. Between the extremes of a heavy viscous oil and a very light oil, there is an infinite variety of crude oil. The manner of producing these crudes is decided only after examining samples that show their characteristics and physical attributes.

Intelligent wells are increasing in popularity. These contain permanent monitoring sensors that measure pressure, temperature, and flow and telemeter these data to the surface. More importantly, these wells contain surface-adjustable downhole flow-control devices, so, based on the dynamic production information from all the wells in the reservoir, flow rates can be optimized without having to perform a costly intervention. [1]

21. WELL COMPLETION

Once the final depth has been reached, the well is completed to allow oil to flow into the casing in a controlled manner. First, a perforating gun is lowered into the well to the production depth.

The gun has explosive charges to create holes in the casing through which oil can flow. After the casing has been perforated, a small-diameter pipe (tubing) is run into the hole as a conduit for oil and gas to flow up the well and a packer is run down the outside of the tubing. When the packer is set at the production level, it is expanded to form a seal around the outside of the tubing. Finally, a multivalve structure is installed at the top of the tubing and cemented to the top of the casing. The Christmas tree allows them to control the flow of oil from the well.

---

[1]Hussein K. Abdel-Aal, Mohammed A. Alsahlawi: Petroleum Economics and Engineering. Third Edition. Taylor & Francis Group, LLC. 2014. P 229:230

Tight formations are occasionally encountered and it becomes necessary to encourage flow.

Several methods are used, one of which involves setting off small explosions to fracture the rock. If the formation is mainly limestone, hydrochloric acid is sent down the hole to dissolve channels in the rock. The acid is inhibited to protect the steel casing. In sandstone, the preferred method is hydraulic fracturing.

A fluid with a viscosity high enough to hold coarse sand in suspension is pumped at very high pressure into the formation, fracturing the rock. The grains of sand remain, helping to hold the cracks open. [1]

After a well has been drilled, it must be completed before oil and gas production can begin. The first step in this process is installing casing pipe in the well.

Oil and gas wells usually require four concentric strings of pipe: conductor pipe, surface casing, intermediate casing, and production casing. The production casing or oil string is the final casing for most wells. The

---

[1] James G. Speight: The Chemistry and Technology of Petroleum. FOURTH EDITION. Taylor & Francis Group, LLC. 2007. P 144:145

production casing completely seals off the producing formation from water aquifers.

The production casing runs to the bottom of the hole or stops just above the production zone. Usually, the casing runs to the bottom of the hole. In this situation the casing and cement seal off the reservoir and prevent fluids from leaving. In this case the casing must be perforated to allow liquids to flow into the well. This is a perforated completion. Most wells are completed by using a perforated completion. Perforating is the process of piercing the casing wall and the cement behind it to provide openings through which formation fluids may enter the wellbore. [1]

While safety and cost are of prime importance in selecting and designing a well completion, the engineer has to consider the following factors in finalizing the completion design:

Type of reservoir and drive mechanisms Rock and fluid properties Need for artificial lift Future needs for stimulation and workover Future needs for enhanced recovery methods

---

[1]Hussein K. Abdel-Aal, Mohammed A. Alsahlawi: Petroleum Economics and Engineering. Third Edition. Taylor & Francis Group, LLC. 2014. P 262

Normally, the technical factors are first considered to determine possible completion designs; then the economic aspects are considered to select the most economical design. [1]

22. Exploring Observed Cognitive Error Types in Teams Working in Simulated Drilling Environments

The environment in which drilling teams work can be characterized as dynamic, uncertain, high-risk, and involves multiple players in often geographically distributed locations. Such conditions therefore require the team to perform safely and effectively to achieve their objectives. Other high hazard industries, such as aviation, healthcare, and maritime, where teams must function in similar circumstances to drilling teams, have increasingly acknowledged the importance of non-technical skills (NTS) [2] and have taken action to investigate, identify, train and assess NTS. [3]

---

[1] Hussein K. Abdel-Aal, Mohammed A. Alsahlawi: Petroleum Economics and Engineering. Third Edition. Taylor & Francis Group, LLC. 2014. P 262:263

[2] non-technical skills

[3] Sacit M. Cetiner • Paul Fechtelkotter Michael Legatt: Advances in Human Factors in Energy: Oil, Gas, Nuclear and Electric Power Industries. Springer International Publishing Switzerland 2017. P 101

Behavioral markers systems include NTS categories and behaviors and provide a framework that can be used to observe non-technical behaviors that contribute to superior or substandard performance within a work environment. Behavioral markers are typically identified specifically for the role or context under examination. For example, behavioral marker systems have been developed in aviation, such as the NOTECHS system for air crew, and in medicine, such as ANTS for anesthetists and NOTSS for surgeons. Behavioral marker systems can provide a basis for designing a curriculum for training NTS, for assessment, and for providing feedback. [1]

In the drilling context, NTS have been receiving relatively recent attention. Following a number of accidents and incidents in the oil and gas industry over the past decade, for example the Deep-Water Horizon tragedy in 2010, there is growing awareness of the impact of NTS on safety and performance. The Energy Institute and also the International Association of Oil and Gas Producers (IOGP) have published guidance on the implementation of Crew Resource Management (CRM) with the aim of providing an overview and learning objectives for non-technical skills training delivery and assessment.

---

[1] Sacit M. Cetiner • Paul Fechtelkotter Michael Legatt: Advances in Human Factors in Energy: Oil, Gas, Nuclear and Electric Power Industries. Springer International Publishing Switzerland 2017. P 102

In order to perform safely and effectively, a drilling team therefore depends on the competencies of individuals as well as the team's. Team competencies refer to the knowledge, skills and attitudes (KSAs) of the team as a whole, that is: what team members think; what team members do, and what team members feel. These KSAs form the basis of the team non-technical skills. [1]

As well as reinforcing the NTS of individual team members through training interventions such as CRM, other high hazard industries, particularly aviation and healthcare, have recognized that the behaviors of the team strongly influence outcomes and therefore safety. Training interventions, especially simulator-based team training, have been developed to stimulate team behaviors in inter-disciplinary teams, which can then be debriefed to improve safe and efficient performance. Team members are encouraged to reflect on their own behaviors as well as those of the team, in particular, team non-technical skills such as team communication, co-operation and co-

---

[1] Sacit M. Cetiner • Paul Fechtelkotter Michael Legatt: Advances in Human Factors in Energy: Oil, Gas, Nuclear and Electric Power Industries. Springer International Publishing Switzerland 2017. P 102

ordination, situational awareness, and decision making. [1]

Specific and directed debriefing and feedback is considered essential to

improving performance but requires a tool or technique to act as a basis for the debrief. The feedback should attempt to strengthen effective habits and behaviors and to modify ineffective ones. Using an error typology which describes the errors in drilling team terms can enhance the learning opportunities from the exercise by highlighting the types of errors that can occur and raising awareness of their impact. Team members can reflect on what they did, how they did it, and why they did it that way, and can generate mitigations for themselves or for the team. [2]

In total, the majority of cognitive errors were observed as being marginally below expectations (67 %) than well below expectations (33 %). This implies that, with focused training objectives, team performance could be improved to avoid or mitigate errors in all three categories. Errors made under Team

---

[1] Sacit M. Cetiner • Paul Fechtelkotter Michael Legatt: Advances in Human Factors in Energy: Oil, Gas, Nuclear and Electric Power Industries. Springer International Publishing Switzerland 2017. P 103
[2] Sacit M. Cetiner • Paul Fechtelkotter Michael Legatt: Advances in Human Factors in Energy: Oil, Gas, Nuclear and Electric Power Industries. Springer International Publishing Switzerland 2017. P 109

Work and Communication were rated almost the same in terms of being well below expectations (16 %) as the other two categories combined (8 and 9 % respectively). This substantiates other research showing that communication failures affecting team functioning are a major contribution to incidents and near misses. Training interventions need to target the types of errors categorized as being well below expectations to improve communication within a drilling team. The errors made under each category were similar but occasional differences did emerge. [1]

The effect of stressors such as uncertainty, time pressure, dynamic events, and multiple non-co-located players were seldom observed during these simulator-based exercises. Although it is not possible to categorically describe why this would be, one potential explanation could be that the exercises were not designed to create stressful situations. These observations took place during a training intervention developed to allow trainees to demonstrate their knowledge and skills, rather than being assessed. In order to observe examples of errors due to team workload and stress management the scenarios would need to

---

[1] Sacit M. Cetiner • Paul Fechtelkotter Michael Legatt: Advances in Human Factors in Energy: Oil, Gas, Nuclear and Electric Power Industries. Springer International Publishing Switzerland 2017. P 109

be modified to include triggers to increase stress. [1]

23. Well Abandonment

The exact timing of cessation of production can be difficult to predict. However, a close working relationship between the reservoir, downhole and salvage engineers should be developed to establish the timing of a well and platform abandonment project. Before abandonment can begin, the salvage engineer must confirm that all wells on the platform are abandoned. The wells should be permanently abandoned according to the recommended procedures of the governing body. Generally, this means isolating productive zones of the well with cement, removing some or all of the production tubing and setting a surface cement plug in the well with the top of the plug approximately 30–50 m below the mudline. The inner casing string should be checked to ensure that adequate diameter and depths are available for the lowering of explosives or cutting tools. If the well plug and abandonment are not performed properly, removal of the conductor by explosive or mechanical means becomes unsafe and much more expensive.

---

[1] Sacit M. Cetiner • Paul Fechtelkotter Michael Legatt: Advances in Human Factors in Energy: Oil, Gas, Nuclear and Electric Power Industries. Springer International Publishing Switzerland 2017. P 109

There are mainly three ways to operate:

1. Using a mobile drill rig

2. Using a platform rig

3. Using a rigless intervention system

To ensure no delays in structure removal, all well plug and abandonments should be completed several months prior to commencement of offshore decommissioning. After well plug and abandonment responsibility and schedules have been established, the next step is an information-gathering phase. According to the latest forecast, in the UK continental Shelf area alone, 930 wells are going to be decommissioned in the next decade. [1]

---

[1] Stefan Orszulik: Environmental Technology in the Oil Industry. Third edition. Springer International Publishing Switzerland 2016. P 264: 265

24. Production Shutdown

A primary objective during the production shutdown is to protect the marine environment and the ecosystem by proper collection, control, transport and disposal of various waste streams. Production shutdown is a dangerous phase of the abandonment operation and creates the possibility of environmental pollution. Shutdown and removal or abandonment in place should be carried out by personnel who have specific knowledge and experience in safety, process flows, platform operations, marine transportation, structural systems and pipeline operations. All contractors involved with the shutdown should be brought in early in the planning stage to further assure a smooth decommissioning project.

The sequence of shutting down the process system, utilities, power supplies and life support systems is important. The platform's power, communications and life support systems should be maintained for as long as practicable to support the decommissioning effort.

Process systems throughout the platform will have to be flushed, purged and degassed in order to remove any trapped hydrocarbons. Safe lock-out, tag-out, hot work and vessel entry procedures must be in place to ensure safety. Procedures must outline all duties of the standby/rescue teams including the use of breathing apparatus, air purging and lighting and caution must be exercised in removing all amounts of gases, oils and solids which may still remain in valves, production headers, filter housings, vessels and pipework that could present hazards to the crew.

Platform decommissioning will result in large amounts of waste liquids and solids. Where possible, waste liquids can be dealt with most cost effectively by placing them in existing pipelines and sending them to existing operating facilities.

If no ongoing operations are available, then the waste streams will have to be pumped into storage containers and transported onshore for disposal or recycling. The constituents of the waste stream will dictate the cost of disposal. Solid wastes such as discarded batteries, glycol filters and absorbent rags will also have to be handled onshore according to acceptable disposal practices. Many platforms will have chemical treatment additives as well as possible toxic/hazardous materials such as methanol, biocides, antifoams, oxygen scavengers, corrosion inhibitors, paints and solvents, some of which may cause damage to the marine environment if accidentally discharged. Therefore, the procedures for handling and containing should be followed. The presence of radioactive scale, NORM, PCBs, hydrogen sulfide, etc., should have been detected during the environmental survey and a disposal plan developed. Disposal will generally mean transporting this material in drums to disposal wells or approved landfills.

Prior to removal, a detailed plan on how each material will be disposed of should be developed. The plan should identify recyclable materials such as steel, rubber and aluminum and the recycling centers that will take delivery of these materials. For those items not to be recycled, the abandonment plan should include the environmental impact that disposal will have on the dump site.

After the process piping and vessels have been cleaned and it has been determined that there is no future utility for the pipelines, pipeline decommissioning should commence. Pipelines departing the platform will either board another platform or commingle with another pipeline via a sub-sea tie-in. A surface to surface decommissioning is the least costly to perform. This requires pigging the line to vacate any residual hydrocarbons followed by flushing with one-line volume of detergent water followed by final rinsing with one-line volume of sea water. Upon completion of the pipeline purging operation, pipeline ends should be cut, plugs inserted and the ends buried below the sea-bed. In the case of a sub-sea tie-in, details of the sub-sea tap will have to be obtained so that pipeline decommissioning plans can be developed. The flowline can be pigged, flushed and disconnected if the receiving platform can accept the fluids, otherwise the pipeline segment will have to be isolated from the adjoining trunkline and then decommissioned. This will generally involve a boat capable of mooring over the sub-sea tie-in, connecting flexible piping to the tie-in using divers or ROVs, then pumping pigs, detergent water and rinsing water toward the platform for handling.

Decommissioning involves a variety of waste streams, disposal handling methods and specialty contractors. This phase more than any other will determine the success of the abandonment and salvage. [1]

Well logging is a continuous recording process of the activities during drilling, well development, and production until the closure of the well. Thus, the record identifies the history of the well. Well logging is carried out during the drilling operation using special probes (electrical resistivity, inductance, or magnetic resonance), physical sampling of the drilled soils and rocks, core samples, monitoring drilling fluid, etc.

---

[1] Stefan Orszulik: Environmental Technology in the Oil Industry. Third edition. Springer International Publishing Switzerland 2016. P 268: 269

Various parameters, such as porosity, permeability, and water saturation in oil, of the formation are also obtained by the resistivity probes. During the drilling operation, information about the drill bit, its movement, and direction are determined by these probes. The direction of drilling is ascertained by the dipole sharing investigation tool (DSI). Information is also gathered to release drill bits stuck in the well, monitoring the perforation operation of the casing to communicate with the formation, the properties of oil and gas in the formation, etc. At various stages of production, well probing is used to inspect the casing, the wall of the uncased well, etc., for necessary maintenance operation of the well. [1]

Oil well logging tools improved after 1947, but the Archie equation is still in use today. When I was consulting on gas wells in New York and Pennsylvania around 1980, I cranked out answers from the Archie equation for each one-foot interval and added up the answers to get the estimated gas reserves for the well. Long before 1980, photographic recording of well logs as wiggly lines had been replaced by computer processing. I asked whether the logging company could get its computer to run off the Archie equation for each foot and keep

---

[1] Uttam Ray Chaudhuri: Fundamentals of Petroleum and Petrochemical Engineering. Taylor and Francis Group. 2011. P 16

cumulating the result like an automobile odometer. The next time I was in upstate New York, the company had programmed an Archie odometer; all I had to do was subtract the odometer "mileage" from the top of an interval from the bottom "mileage." I could still use my judgment to pick the top and bottom of a productive interval, but I could get the reserves from a single subtraction. [1]

---

[1] K E N N E T H S . D E F F E Y E S: Hubbert's Peak. Princeton University Press. 2001. P 76: 77

References

1. Alan K. Burnham: Global Chemical Kinetics of Fossil Fuels. Springer International Publishing AG 2017.
2. Andre´ Dorsman • Timur Go¨k • Mehmet Baha Karan: Perspectives on Energy Risk. Springer-Verlag Berlin Heidelberg 2014.
3. C.J. Campbell: Campbell's Atlas of Oil and Gas Depletion. Colin J. Campbell and Alexander Wöstmann 2013.
4. Chidozie Izuchukwu Princeton Dim: Hydrocarbon Prospectivity in the Eastern Coastal Swamp Depo-belt of the Niger Delta Basin. 2017.
5. Congrui Jin • Gianluca Cusatis: New Frontiers in Oil and Gas Exploration. Springer International Publishing Switzerland 2016.
6. Dawei SUN, Xiaorong XIE, Jianfeng WANG, Qiang LI, Che WEI: Integrated generation-transmission expansion planning for offshore oilfield power systems based on genetic Tabu hybrid algorithm. J. Mod. Power Syst. Clean Energy. 2017.
7. Ellis H.Austin: Drilling Engineering, International Human Resources Development Corporation • Boston D. Reidel Publishing Company, 1983.
8. François Roure • Ammar A. Amin Sami Khomsi • Mansour A.M. Al Garni: Lithosphere Dynamics and Sedimentary Basins of the Arabian Plate and Surrounding Areas. Springer International Publishing AG 2017.

9. Frank Jahn, Mark Cook and Mark Graham: HYDROCARBON EXPLORATION AND PRODUCTION. 2ND EDITION. Elsevier B.V. 2008.
10. Georgios M. Kopanos · Pei Liu Michael C. Georgiadis: Advances in Energy Systems Engineering. Springer International Publishing Switzerland 2017.
11. Hongqi Liu: Principles and Applications of Well Logging, Petroleum Industry Press, china 2017.
12. Hussein K. Abdel-Aal Mohamed A. Aggour Mohamed A. Fahim: Petroleum and Gas Field Processing. Second Edition. Taylor & Francis Group, LLC. 2016.
13. Hussein K. Abdel-Aal, Mohammed A. Alsahlawi: Petroleum Economics and Engineering. Third Edition. Taylor & Francis Group, LLC. 2014.
14. Investments in exploration/production and refining 2015. IFP Energies Nouvelles - January 2016.
15. James G. Speight: The Chemistry and Technology of Petroleum. FOURTH EDITION. Taylor & Francis Group, LLC. 2007.
16. JOHN CUBITT: Handbook of Petroleum Exploration and Production. Elsevier Science B.V. 2002.
17. KENNETH S. DEFFEYES: Hubbert's Peak. Princeton University Press. 2001.
18. Kun Sang Lee • Tae Hong Kim: Integrative Understanding of Shale Gas Reservoirs. 2016.

19. Mark J.Kaiser, Brian F.Snyder: The Offshore Drilling Industry and Rig Construction in the Gulf of Mexico, Springer-Verlag London 2013.
20. MIHIR K. SINHA, LARRY R. PADGETT: RESERVOIR ENGINEERING TECHNIQUES USING FORTRAN. D. Reidel Publishing Company 1985.
21. Nick Bahrami: Evaluating Factors Controlling Damage and Productivity in Tight Gas Reservoirs. Doctoral Thesis. Springer International Publishing Switzerland 2013.
22. Patrick A. Narbel • Jan Petter Hansen Jan R. Lien: Energy Technologies and Economics. Springer International Publishing Switzerland 2014.
23. R.L.Sengbush: petroleum exploration, a quantitative introduction, library of congress 1st edition 1986.
24. Ripudaman Malhotra: Fossil Energy. Springer Science+Business Media New York 2013.
25. Robert Ayres: ENERGY, COMPLEXITY AND WEALTH MAXIMIZATION. Springer International Publishing Switzerland 2016.
26. Sacit M. Cetiner • Paul Fechtelkotter Michael Legatt: Advances in Human Factors in Energy: Oil, Gas, Nuclear and Electric Power Industries. Springer International Publishing Switzerland 2017.
27. Sanjib Chowdhury: Optimization and Business Improvement Studies in Upstream Oil and Gas Industry. John Wiley & Sons, Inc. 2016.

28. Stefan Orszulik: Environmental Technology in the Oil Industry. Third edition. Springer International Publishing Switzerland 2016.
29. Uttam Ray Chaudhuri: Fundamentals of Petroleum and Petrochemical Engineering. Taylor and Francis Group. 2011.

Biography of the author

Roshdy Ebrahim Abdin, Egyptian.

Ph.D (ECONOMICS)

Economic lecturer.

Member at the Egyptian assembly for political economy.

Member at the Egyptian assembly for international law.

Master degree in economic law.

Professional diploma in arbitration.

Professional diploma in importing and exporting.

Lawyer since 2008.

For more information please subscribe to my blog:

http://roshdyebrahim.blogspot.com.eg/

www.ingramcontent.com/pod-product-compliance
Lightning Source LLC
Chambersburg PA
CBHW031615210526
45464CB00004B/1586